Low-Power Sorting Architectures for FPGA Systems

AF872225

BY

Chin Peing

TABLE OF CONTENTS

Chapter 1

Introduction

Hardware accelerators is the process of an application offloads certain computing activities onto dedicated hardware within the system. It provides increased efficiency and performance when using a single general-purpose CPU. Hardware accelerators has great impact on the operations which effects the speed of process. However, considering the case of non-blocking accelerators there is another layer of concurrency in the system. Designing hardware used as accelerators is quite a different domain from software design, the reason behind this is hardware requires massive concurrent working within the accelerator and results in faster execution. Hence considerations by software engineers' impact on different level of concurrency compared to hardware design.

Hardware accelerator finds application in various areas like data analytics, artificial intelligence, robotics and Internet of Things (IoT). IoT concepts will have a very high influence in our daily life in the near future. IoT will permeate every part of our life and most of the products and services, human beings consume will be influenced by the idea of IoT. IoT aims to seamlessly integrate the physical and digital world in order to build things in network. The Internet of Things will dramatically affect few of the sectors like agriculture, industry, and services. Due to this, IoT is also described as Industrial Revolution 4.0 [1].

The physical objects are getting computational and wireless communication capabilities. This results in network of smart objects which exchange information and interact without human intervention. The network of smart objects is called IoT. Several technologies like high speed networking, distributed storage, cloud computing play an enabling and important role in realization of IoT [2]. At the edge layer or in data centre, hardware accelerators can be deployed for fast processing of data.

Across the different layers/hierarchies of IoT, there is a limited interoperability for data transactions. Researchers both in academia and industry are developing IoT applications with data science. Designing high speed data dissemination systems is a challenge for IoT applications which use modern data analytics [3]. There is a necessity for the systems which cope up with the speed of the internet and cater to needs of modern data analytics in real time. This problem must be addressed at different layers of IoT ecosystem. The large amount of data is accumulated from different sources like IoT edge nodes, web pages and social networks [4]. The advanced algorithms are used to analyze the data which are useful in emerging applications like customized advertisement and user behavior mining etc [5].

The data center infrastructure of service providers across the applications of IT industry requires a complete overhaul of both software and hardware [6]. Development of new algorithms and processing hardware or CPU for data intensive applications in IoT is an open research problem. The performance of CPU is saturating, also the end of Moore's law and further increasing the performance of CPU is a big concern [7]. Along with performance, the energy is also a dominant limiting factor in current day data intensive applications [6]. At different layers of IoT, from data centres (cloud layer) to edge/perception layer, bigdata workloads expose lacuna in processing capabilities of general purpose CPUs [6].

1.1 Hardware Accelerators

Hardware acceleration combines the advantage of both software and hardware. The software components provide efficiency and adaptability of general-purpose processors by deploying hardware resources such as GPUs and ASICs. These resources increase efficiency by higher magnitude when implemented on digital computing systems. For instance, visualization process can be offloaded onto a graphics card to enable speed, improved quality of playback videos and games, by this offloading mechanism the CPU can now be used for other activities.

There is a lot of advantages using both hardware and software for an application. The decision of executing an application made by a designer, partitioning the program execution with minimal interaction among hardware and software is paramount. Thus, while utilizing both hardware and software care should be taken such that every unit is busy and no components are idle. This provides the opportunity to work concurrently and executes fast.

A variety of hardware accelerators available on shelf. The best example is tethering accelerator, like WiFi hotspot which enables the offload operations on chip results in workload balancing and increases energy efficiency.

Hardware accelerator technologies are embraced to overcome the performance concerns of general purpose CPUs. Hardware-software co-design techniques to share the load between CPU and accelerators are investigated in recent times to find out the apt solutions. Hardware accelerators are a new and promising method for increasing the processing elements speed. The optimal utilization of computing resources like Arithmetic and logic Units (ALUs), floating point and customized units is possible by inclusion of accelerators with main CPU.

Accelerators can be implemented as ASICs (Application Specific Integrated Circuits), FPGA (Field Programmable Gate Arrays) and GPGPUs (General Purpose Graphics Processing Units). Each of these implementations will come with their own advantages and challenges. Generally, accelerators implemented in any of these methods attain higher performance than using CPU alone [20].

Graphics Processing Unit (GPU) also known as hardware acceleration for graphics which works on server-side by streaming video and enabling modern Application Programming Interface (API) for interactive visualizations of data. Another type of hardware acceleration is using Artificial Intelligence (AI) for the application such as neural networks, machine vision, robotics and Internet of Things.

The GPU architecture overview given in general and describes the data-parallel programming methods like OpenCL [5] and CUDA for the GPU section. Then, attention paid to NVIDIA's GPU and outline essential CUDA toolkit capabilities using part of the code and illustrates for kernel database operations including hashing, sorting, and joins.

Hardware accelerators include:

- Graphics Processing Units (GPUs): actually designed for handling the image motion, but now GPUs can also be used for calculating massive amount of data and accelerating the part of an application mean while the rest of applications run on CPU. The capability of GPU is handling massive amount of records instantly.

- Field Programmable Gate Arrays (FPGAs): the programming like hardware description language (HDL) is best chosen design for semiconductor integrated circuit allowing user to configure electronic components. The major functionality of FPGA is hardware-software co-design allows sharing between FPGA and CPU.
- Application-Specific Integrated Circuits (ASICs): an integrated circuit exclusively used in a particular employment, improves the overall speed of the function. But the complexity of ASICs is huge, since it should handle 100 million logic gates.

Acceleration can also achieve by following different ways:

1. Data parallelism: it is the concurrent using several processor cores to complete the same task. An extensive family of parallel algorithms can be expressed using the powerful programming model known as irregular nested data-parallelism. However, producing efficient code from such programmes for contemporary parallel systems is challenging. On the other hand, regular data-parallelism is considerably simpler to turn into fast code but is too limited to represent some problems conveniently or in a way to fully utilise the parallelism. Single Instruction Multiple Data (SIMD) is associated with hardware acceleration mechanism to achieve data parallelism and exploits spatial parallelism.
2. Task parallelism: Task parallelism is a technique used in parallel computing settings to distribute computer code over a number of processors. Commonly named as control parallelism and function parallelism. The main goal of task parallelism is to divide tasks, concurrently carried out by processes or threads across various processors. Implementation-wise, task parallelism is a potent technique for enhancing performance. However, there may be a wide range in how well the dataflow pragma works when applied to a particular or random piece of

code. To understand the final implementation of the dataflow pragma, it is frequently essential to look at the execution pattern of the individual jobs.

3. Pipeline parallelism: When several processes are interdependent but their execution can overlap, this procedure is noted as pipeline parallelism. The output of one step is streamed as input to the next phase. CPUs frequently use the pipeline method to accelerate processing throughput. It is especially common in code that uses file (or network) accesses; as they compete for various resources, they frequently function well with CPU-intensive computation. CPUs frequently use the pipeline method to accelerate processing throughput. It is extremely prevalent in code that uses file (or network) accesses; as they compete for various resources, they frequently function well with CPU-intensive computation. Pipeline techniques is employed for instruction execution and exploits temporal parallelism.

   Pipeline parallelism allows for the sequential execution of complicated functionality without affecting performance. In this situation, usage of FPGAs in the pipeline stages may communicate effectively. Reason behind effective communication is parameters like close near vicinity and on-chip memory availability in order to build buffers [122].

4. Co-processor design: it is an auxiliary computer processor used to adjunct the capabilities of the processor (CPU). This type of processor is capable of performing a variety of functions, including precision based calculations, digital signal processing, string related operations, graphical algorithm, security based function, and interaction with external devices including input and output accessories. Coprocessors can improve system efficiency by offloading processor-heavy activities from the primary processor. Coprocessors make it possible to modify a line of computers, saving money for users who don't want the added performance.

   In today's embedded system, microprocessor cores are frequently used as the primary component. Since they are made to expand general purpose code, they frequently lack the essential performance to offer all the functionalities needed by applications with a high priority on performance. Due to this, general purpose processors are increasingly being accompanied by a variety of specialised components called accelerators in computation systems. Figure 1.1 depicts the placement of hardware accelerators as a co-processor.

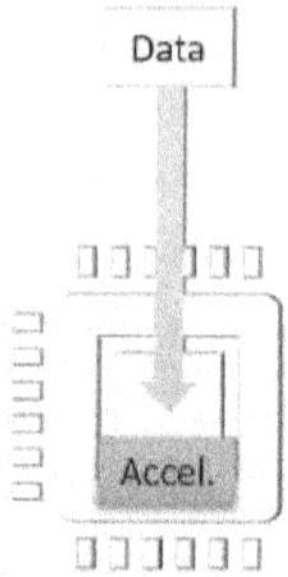

Figure 1.1 Hardware Accelerators as Co-Processor

5. Co-placement design: Placing accelerator on the path of data is the concept of co-placement design. The description of a data path accelerator with configurable parity, length, and extent groups. The data path accelerator has a storage interface for talking to one or more hard drives and a network interface for connecting to one or more clients. It is essential to co-optimize data placement and compute scheduling to maximise data reuse and bandwidth consumption. Applicable for both on- and off-chip memory accesses in order to achieve excellent performance with heterogeneous compute systems equipped with FPGAs. However, it is a difficult task to optimise the data arrangement for FPGA accelerators. Figure 1.2 represents the placement of accelerators in data path.

The major goal of deploying the accelerator in the data channel is to keep the processor's data transfer bandwidth high. This deployment helps to condense the amount of data being transferred to it. Ibex has an FPGA installed that provides a variety of functionalities. This feature incorporated into MySQL strategies in addition to a Solid State Drives (SSD) and a CPU.

The data must still be processed in batches that are large enough to justify the latency overhead and transported through a network (equivalent to an interconnect). There are many acceleration facilities provided by data-path accelerators as well as there are few counterparts encountered. The delay caused by FPGA device is the same intensity as a request made to access socket memory. This overhead is significantly reduced and new opportunities arise when FPGAs are used as co-processors.

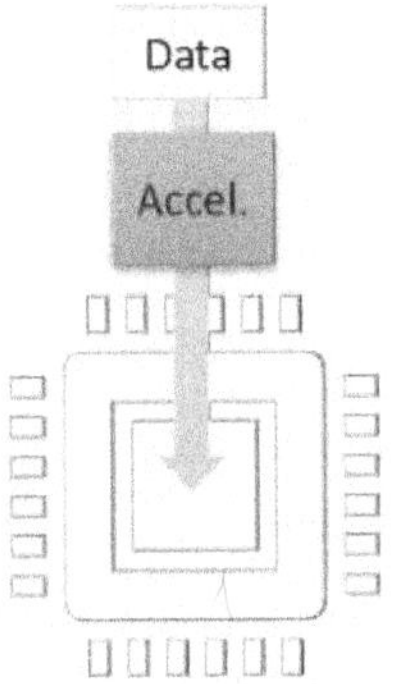

Figure 1.2 Hardware Accelerators in data path

1.2 FPGA vs ASIC

In today's era, there is a great demand for computational speed in terms of data processing on a processor. There is no guarantee that the data processing on CPU is the best and efficient solution. FPGAs are used in the computing world like machine learning, embedded systems, Cloud Computing, and internet of things. Field Programmable Gate Arrays (FPGAs) are widely used as well for security purpose and computational device. FPGAs can be considered as blooming accelerator for new applications. Some of the methodology addressed in [8] [9] like memory interconnection, design tools available in FPGA. There is an improvement set required for FPGA to excel the computation using database operations. Such a tremendous feature of FPGA for in-memory data application brings a great success of using as edge device.

The major differences between FPGA and ASIC by considering parameters like cost, power consumption, memory and reusability are discussed in this section.

FPGA consists of a reconfigurable component that helps in extending the flexibility of programming and improving performance of hardware by reinforcing parallelism. Such an advantage of FPGA platform enabled a huge amount of computations to be considered concurrently, alleviating the sequential components. The instructions given to processor are the directions given to process data. There is another important gain achieved using FPGAs is its capability to process streamed data at wire speed with a minimal access to memory. The mentioned benefits of FPGAs being communicated with ASIC. However, the reconfiguration capability of FPGAs are adjustable to changes in applications and resulting faster time to market.

FPGAs can also be used for data conversion and is not visible for the user but when brought to the front line of processing, they have better ability to offload processing power from the CPU. This enables high bandwidths that can be easily managed.

FPGAs can also be used in security aspects. In FASTEN [117], cloud computing platforms has the hardware that is separated from the main computer system. The data process takes place in kernel code that is put into action. The FPGA fabric has been updated with the kernel code. The data processing and cryptography are carried out with in the hardware. This is practically infeasible pathways due to exposure of plaintext data. Additionally, this platform uses the modern FPGAs' tamper-resistant features in order to resist against side-channel attacks such Differential Power Analysis (DPA). There are few security features that are combined with FPGAs' flexibility to employ them in the cloud.

The sensitive parts of applications are executed on FPGAs in [118]. Cryptography for the FPGA configuration is the best solution during deployment. The strategy, nevertheless, is reliant on the Trusted Authority's core management.

FPGAs have shown its success in accelerating database queries like sorting, selecting, join, hashing, projection and so on. This success is compared with databases implemented using MySQL and Postgres. The reason behind this is the fact that many early FPGA-deployed database acceleration initiatives recommend using them as auxiliary accelerators for row storage [33] [123] [124]. However, the advantages are much minimized if the price of connection over Peripheral Component Interconnect (PCIe) and the cost of the software required to prepare the data for the FPGA are taken into account.

The intrinsic flexibility of fine-grained parallelism of FPGA offers a massive data task, pipelining, parallelism totally results in faster execution on data. Because of their non-instruction design and programmable logic units, FPGAs may implement combinational and sequential logic. They also offer low-latency data processing. The advantage here is prototype of the hardware remains same but the circuit keeps changing using HDL. The ratio of high performance and low power consumptions satisfied by FPGA accelerators.

FPGAs are usually a set of logic building components consisting of logic cells, I/O cells and connecting the resources. The advancement made on FPGA hardware technology remodeled and customized as per user/programmer requirement. Processor components used are oscillator, DRAM, clock generator, floating-point units, drivers, bus interconnector and controllers are now part of a multicore processors. Further all these devices can be replaced by FPGA with supporting languages including languages such as C, C++ and OpenCL have made better result acting as an accelerator in addition to Verilog.

1.3 Features of FPGAs

FPGAs as accelerator can be used in data centers and also in the sectors like IOT edge devices, automatic driving, and robotics and in application requiring low tolerance of telecommunication delays. Given limited battery service and low cost on big servers, FPGA is a superior option for applications demanding large scale data processes.

The primary reason of heterogeneous platforms is to employ compute-intensive applications. FPGAs has capability and featured with improved throughput, reconfigurable and energy-efficient mechanisms for huge block or stream of data. Two kind of parallelism featured by FPGAs: firstly, parallelism using pipeline concepts- little complex, but throughput achieved.

FPGAs main benefit is that the interconnection between sequence of pipeline stages is effective. Due to their physical proximity and accessibility to on-chip memory that serves as FIFO buffers finds place for FPGA. Secondly, FPGAs in data-parallel execution, same as single instruction multiple data (SIMD) processed in CPU. Hence, the acceleration fact of FPGAs is interesting due to the parallelism feature.

In the modern era, data abundance is inevitable and the rate of data increase is exponential. To handle such abundant data, an improved CPU core is required. Even by increasing the CPU-core count does not power up the efficiency in handling database operations, resulting in CPU process limitation [10]. This limitation on the field of in-memory database management demands for the need of the methodologies to gain up the rate of database operations. Field-Programmable Gate Arrays (FPGAs) methodology provides consistent among the growing technologies. FPGA supports immense parallelism and enhance the computational performance. Another feature regarding FPGA which makes flexible operations on database by reconfiguring circuit. It also improves the accessibility of input/output device and reduces the power consumption of each operation. This is achieved by attaching FPGA with CPU. So FPGA can be considered as a candidate for the design of an accelerator.

In data analytics related applications, FPGA serves as an accelerator device. This research cited many among the most recent studies that explained the competence of using FPGA as in-memory accelerator in terms of high bandwidth and throughput. The necessity of the in-memory accelerator on data path and its impact is well explained in IBM [11].

In aforesaid IBM accelerator, FPGA is used for accelerating two steps of decompression and pre-processing between the dataflow of HDD and CPU. This betterment reduces the computational overhead of the CPU which blindly limits the usage and amplified the bandwidth connected to the data analytics performance. Even though the high parallelism and intrinsic nature speed up the power of kernel load of CPU in low interface bandwidth, the blockage of such research allied to high bandwidth in-memory database are still left void.

The reason being overshadow of the accelerator FPGA in excess of main memory is the economic constraints even with the increased benefits. The challenge on system speedup is left obvious with least emerging technologies handling the situation with less computation which reduces the overall cost and non-linear pathways. Some of the successful in-memory interface technologies with higher bandwidth working capability are Compute Express Link (CXL) [13], Cache Coherent Interconnect for Accelerators (CCIX) [12], Coherent Accelerator Processor Interface (CAPI) [12] [14], etc.

One of the important features of FPGA that makes the acceleration more consequential is shared memory. In most of the existing systems, FPGA is chosen as IO device controlled by the CPU rather than open architecture because of hardware coherence. The shared memory space peers the FPGA over the existing CPU [15]. The FPGAs are accessed by the shared memory capabilities to store a significant amount of data locally. Therefore, reducing the total number of host memory retrieval and perhaps accelerating some data-intensive programmes that need to access memory repeatedly. This research paper reviews the FPGA's potential and its significant performance appraisal considering acceleration features of in-memory database systems. The contributions obtained from this review are made on three uncertainties. They are

i) FPGA architectural alternatives with the restricted access on any type of CPU system core with the analysis.

ii) In-memory trends and reconsideration possibilities.

iii) State-of-art research methodologies categorized on procedures such as:

a) Architectural level approach: the performance of database operation in FPGA is based on the architectural overview of the DBMS layers. There are many supporting architecture in FPGA used by researchers such as in-memory based accelerator, parallelism architecture, on-fly data movement architecture, offloading queries and customized query architecture.

b) Partitioning approach: this approach occurs when there is random memory sharing access and time consuming as joining process is involved. This approach also effects the performance held between the FPGA and CPU during the data movement.

c) Constructive approach: in this approach a multi-algorithm hybridization technique for effective in-memory acceleration on FPGA is proposed by researchers.

d) Joining approach: one of the important operation on FPGA is join. There are various types of join operation like hash join, merge join etc.

e) Boosting approach: mainly to speed up the overall performance of in-memory operations carried out by FPGA.

f) Divisive approach: The dividing strategy is a hierarchical approach that uses an agglomerative clustering procedure to speed up database memory operations.

g) Distributive approach: DBMS workload is distributed across all service tiers using a distributive technique.

Generally, Relational database management systems (RDBMS) are well known for storing data. The responses to requests are made easier in the form of SQL queries. This system also provides capability to analyze and process the data. Developing efficient processing of query techniques for high speed and reduced power consumption is required for modern IoT era and also for functioning of data centers cost effectively. Hardware accelerators are promising solutions which can be deployed in data centers and also in the different hierarchies of IoT for time effective and cost effective query processing.

1.4 Motivation

Internet of Things (IoT) deployment success mostly rely on efficient data processing and drawing relevant conclusions from gathered data having minimal latency. Big data analytics experiences emerged as a result of the need to crunch data. Big data analytics related to contemporary business data occupy a sizable amount of database tuples. As well big data analytics computer systems in the IoT era require high computation ability due to its continuous data generation. This typically can be achieved through multi-core processing systems, which has triggered advanced research in heterogeneous computing. Hence forth in traditional database systems and contemporary big data analytics, sorting has become a crucial activity [16]. Numerous applications, such as data analytics, artificial intelligence, data mining, digital signal processing, scientific computing, cloud computing, high energy physics, etc., require sorting operations [17] [18].

Sorting is a basic operation performed by the queries in the applications that require data access. Data sorting plays a vital role in the applications like IOT perception layers, data processing centres, data extraction, IOT edge nodes, and servers in order to process the query. The main advantage of sorting is to extract the data easily out of database, since the data required will be in the alphabetical or numerical order list. For several sorting algorithms, exploration have been accomplished using software approach as well on hardware devices like ASIC or FPGA. As investigated by various researchers, software approach is easy to handle and carry out. Sorting can also be performed on hardware device, results comparatively high performance but configuring and executing query is unwieldy.

In most of the sorting techniques, data attributes like data size, data element count, speed and time are taken into account while evaluating performance. In this section, review of the existing techniques related to hardware sorters on FPGAs presented.

Field Programmable Gate Array (FPGA) is a reconfigurable component and allow consumers to reprogram. Nowadays industries are moving from bandwidth based to compute intensive based, the FPGA finds its place in compute intensive applications. Internally FPGAs consists of LUTs, local memory, configurable interconnect fabric and small processing unit which provides benefit of reprogramming.

1.5 Research Problem

Both software and hardware can implement sorting [19]. Sorting is the common operation performed when speed is the requirement and sorting in hardware are feasible. As it's known that the majority of IoT application requires high performance and efficient big data analytics. Sorting processes in software implementation use an excessive amount of CPU cycles, according to many data analytics researchers [19]. To obtain high speed sorting techniques, accelerators like dedicated ASIC or FPGA can be used to fulfill performance attainment [19] [21]. The suitable architecture of hardware sorting units is equipped on the target applications with few constraints like number of inputs, width of inputs and energy consumption. Nowadays both industry and academia researchers attracted towards designing efficient hardware sorting techniques [21] [22].

The recent sorting techniques mainly concentrate on enhancing computational and effective energy management. Majority of the hardware sorting methodology implemented in ASIC or FPGA use merge sorter, bubble sorter, bitonic sorter and odd-even sorter [22]. Hardware sorting implementation are comparatively suitable for small set of elements known in prior, whereas software implementation suitable for dynamic set of elements. There is a lot of good research work done on FPGA sorting technique implementations and researchers now much attracted towards the novel FPGA implementations for sorting data sets since it supports sequential instructions and hence parallelism can be easily achieved on a reconfigurable hardware [23] [24] [25].

In recent decades, the servers at data centers has changed drastically to handle massive data. There are several computing devices like multi-core processors, Graphical processor units, FPGAs and other hardware accelerators are playing important role at data centers serving different level of applications. These esoteric hardware accelerators in data centers shows a better performance, reduction in computational latency and response time in an application [26] [27].

Another trending research on going in contemporary data center is lowering the power usage during computation and as well thermal cooling is a concern [27] [28] [29]. The usage of internet is high, which creates greater demand of data computation at data centers and also corresponding power consumption has also increased.

Generally sorting operations on data, consumes extra power. The researchers are paying attention on illustrating novel method which consumes low-power without affecting how efficiently the sorting processes work. There are many combinations of heterogeneous device models used with FPGA. Example models are CPU-GPU and CPU-FPGA in data centers. Even so FPGA has certain advantageous feature for sorting operations like reconfiguring capability, ease of parallel implementation, fast and efficient in computation etc. There are certain drawbacks: -

- In contrast to ASIC implementations, the challenge is to design a low-power computing components without sacrificing performance using FPGAs. It is more difficult with FPGAs because the devices are already manufactured.
- In ASIC designs, there is an effective control over the trade-off caused between power and performance utilising low power management techniques. Power gating and Dynamic Voltage Frequency Scaling (DVFS) are popular low power techniques, which might not be supported over all FPGA devices that were at the disposal.

Presently, FPGAs are deployed in cloud data centers. To process huge data sets in cloud are now deployed with enormous count of FPGAs to accomplish the requisite over performance. Another factor is power consumption that has become a significant gridlock for further improvement [24] [27]. Ultimately, very soon or later ASIC in servers will be replaced by FPGA that requires balancing between power and performance [16] [27].

1.6 Research Objectives

As discussed above, one of the primary element for computation in data centers is sorting engine and it's a highlighted fact that researchers are now concentrated mainly on designing the sorting models on FPGA devices. Comparatively less exposure has been done on ASIC devices for implementing sorting algorithms than on FPGAs. Now the challenge is to design low power sorting technique suitable to data centers without compromising the performance. There are many low power techniques in digital world, among them few efficient methods are clock gating, power gating, and Dynamic Voltage Frequency Scaling (DVFS). DVFS can be widely imposed on sorting techniques like bitonic sorting, odd-even sorting, and bubble sorting.

An open research challenge is the exploration of scheme trade-offs between power and throughput of various low power sorting engines. This study mainly focuses on clock gating to obtain low power in sorting engines. And also presents the findings of a power performance trade-off for popular sorting methods. There are few attraction towards FPGAs, they have a privilege of processing high level parallelism (task and data), low latency, low power consumption and can also be used as an accelerator in many applications [30].

The hardware sorter based on merge sort technique proposed in [31], resulted in improvement of throughput by 3.13x times than traditional method. But the proposed method in [31] requires more number of comparators and hence causes resource scarcity.

[32] Proposed a tree based merge sorter for large-scale sorting and successfully implemented, but there was a degradation of performance for distorted data. A reliable approach implemented using sort-merge units [33] improved throughput, unfortunately failed to scale for large number of data items. This paper provides detailed comparison of various sorting technique. The parameter that is emphasized in this paper is comparator-free sorting. Many research carried out for comparator-free sorting drawing attention towards speed and resource utilization. Usually the proposed technique does not use any sort of comparators or complex data path [34].

In the current trends, microprocessors are available commercially in market and with this technology RISC based systems like ARM, Atmel-AVR are available for the embedded systems. These devices are widely used in various applications including IoT edge devices and in energy constrained systems [9]. RISC-V provides a flexibility to develop instruction set suitable for embedded systems and many researchers contributed for the same. This support of RISC-V attempts to successful collaboration of industries throughout the globe. This feature provides flexibility in using the open license and new instructions can be used anywhere [35]. This has aided research groups in developing unique approaches for modifying the RISC-V architecture, which has resulted in a hardware accelerator.

The CPU, decoder, General Purpose Registers (GPR), Control and Status Register (CSR), ALU, Multiplier, and many other key parts make up the RISC-V architecture. Prefetch is a significant sections of CPU. The process carried out in Prefetch section is deciphers the commands from memory and it exhibits the received instructions to the other blocks. Its well-known that sorting is a basic prefetch operation performed by any application. Notably, sorting plays a crucial role by assisting queries during the process and there worth techniques for sorting operations in hardware which is been witnessed in data centers, mining, edge devices and cloud servers [36].

Sorting is primary operation performed while accessing data from database, as the data needed will be in alpha-numerical order. Therefore, an optimized hardware sorting algorithm is required that can accelerate the performance of data analytics. Normally, the sorter algorithms will be first tested in software and then verified on hardware device. As FPGA supports reconfigurable feature enabling user to program frequently and in a required manner i.e. customized mode. These features of FPGA finds wide application requiring intensified domains with complex computations. LUTs, memory units, processing units are the primary blocks of FPGA device and as well provides ease of programming [37].

Hardware accelerator finds its importance in parallel computing for high processing, low latency, low power consumption and diverse applications. In past few decades, several different sorting algorithms have been designed for hardware and also tested for various applications. There is a lot of scope to modify the sorter unit as well as finds usage in various real time applications. It is a known fact that the sketched algorithm can be easily tested on software platform. However, demonstrating on a hardware platform with results in comparison of relative performance assessment is doable, but configuring and executing it is time-consuming. The parameters considered for comparison of optimized sorting algorithm are size of data, number of data elements, speed and time.

The research objectives are listed as follows:

1. Design a low power sorter architecture using structured low power techniques like Clock gating and Multi-Vth.
2. Design High Performance Sorters using Low Power circuit/Architectures and Comparison-Free Sorting Architectures
3. Design a customized instruction set for sorting applications in RISC-V microprocessor.

1.7 Thesis Organization

The rest in this thesis is organized into the subsequent sections. Chapter 2 covers a state-of-the-art comprehensive literature review of existing various sorting techniques. Chapter 3 addresses the lower power design using two important structured techniques like clock gating and Multi-Vth. Chapter 4 describes the hardware-based comparison-free odd-even sorting technique. The detailed architecture of the novel sorting in RISC-V and its result analysis represents the subject of Chapter 5. Finally, Chapter 6 states the thesis final conclusion, and Chapter 7 discusses the possible work ahead.

Chapter 2

State-of-the-Art Review

The three basic concepts of any hardware accelerators are power, energy and area. The power usage of FPGAs are attributed for two sub components: static and dynamic power [129]. The main contribution of static power is the power leakage. The impact of FPGA-based accelerators on the design of dynamic power consumption for a given system is another crucial consideration.

2.1 Power, energy and area

The power consumed by circuits during idle state is known as static power. Generally, static power leads to leakage current. Static power is a generally consistent property of a certain device does not depend on input conditions or capacitance. The leakage current can be measured as current flow through the transistors in idle state. This can be observed by considering transistor attributes.

Dynamic power is the amount of energy used by the transistors, passed through circuit when there is a change in states. Transistors in digital CMOS circuits use the greatest power during this transition period because the maximum current is flowing through them. Increased clock frequencies often equate to higher energy utilization in synchronous digital circuits since the majority of energy is used during clock transitions. Clocking the logic as infrequently as feasible is one way to reduce power usage.

By parallelizing portions of the application's duties so that more work is done per clock cycle and decreasing the clock rate, one might potentially reduce the amount of dynamic power that an FPGA design uses. Dynamic power is heavily dependent on the clock frequency. Only when the power saved by lowering the clock rate is more than the power absorbed by the additional logic needed to parallelize the task is the total power lowered.

Hardware accelerators can be useful in a various parameter other than area to improve performance. Hardware accelerators are an additional power-saving device. If adding hardware accelerators to your system improves performance while maintaining the same clock frequency, adding hardware accelerators also preserves the initial performance while reducing the clock frequency. A higher performance can be exchanged for power savings because of the tight correlation between clock frequency and power usage.

A single hardware accelerator can frequently result in significant power savings over a processor alone, but sometimes adding numerous accelerators can further save power. Because adding a lot of inefficient hardware can actually decrease the system's power efficiency rather than increase it, it is even more crucial to consider the architecture of the complete system to allow numerous accelerators. For instance, if numerous accelerators are arbitrating for the same system resource continuously, the efficiency benefit of having multiple accelerators may be offset by the shared resource's excessive use.

More heat is produced by higher power usage, and electronics are harmed by heat. An electronic circuit may malfunction or perhaps get permanently damaged if the temperature is too high [104]. The simple equation (2.1) that follows shows how much power the CPU consumes (P_{CPU}):

$$P_{CPU} = \underbrace{\alpha \times C \times V_{dd}^2 \times f_{clk}}_{\text{dynamic power}} + \underbrace{V_{dd} \times I_{leak}}_{\text{static power}} \tag{2.1}$$

Where C - capacitance at the load (F)

V_{dd} – operating voltage (V)

f_{clk} - clock frequency (Hz)

I_{leak} - current leakage (A)

Ignore other components of power dissipation which are very negligible and are due to current from short circuits and glitches. The important two elements that are most crucial: dynamic power and static power. The energy used when transistors are switching, or when they change states, is referred to as dynamic power. Parameter quantifies the switching activity. Another important power parameter is static power. It is the amount of power dissipated even when the transistors are not in use since they contribute for small magnitude of current leakage (I_{leak}).

The static power experiences current leakage from transistor when they are within a static configuration, is a feature of CMOS-based devices that is generally constant (standby). The majority of the power consumed by transistors comes from the dynamic power, which results from the current that passes through them when they change states [2]. The equation (2.2) provides [130]:

$$\text{Dynamic Power} = C_t V_s^2 f_s A_f \tag{2.2}$$

Where C_t - capacitance of the transistor (F)

V_s- supply voltage (V)

f_s - switching frequency (Hz)

A_f - activity/switching factor

Power calculations must take both static and dynamic power into account. Although FPGA manufacturers are dedicated to offering devices with minimal power consumption, as process technologies advance from 130nm to 90nm to 65nm and beyond, transistors feature size reduces become leakier by nature, increasing static power utilization. Furthermore, the dynamic power utilization of systems embedded with FPGAs increases as a function of frequency and switching node count due to the exceptionally high performance requirements of these systems.

Since parasitic capacitance is constantly being charged and discharged, heat caused by dynamic power adds for the majority of loss in power align with recent FPGAs [105]. The power consumption is given by equation (2.3).

$$P_{avg} = \frac{1}{2} \sum_{n \in nets} C_n \cdot f_n \cdot V^2 \tag{2.3}$$

where P_{avg} - average power consumption (W)

C_n- n net capacitance (F)

V - supply voltage (V)

f_n - average toggle rate of net n (Hz)

Each capacitance and net's switching activity are required as two factors for the equation used to estimate power.

Multicore scaling is filled with issues. Firstly, how much parallelism can be utilized for a given operation now directly affects performance. It's clear from Amdahl's law that if a computation's fraction f is increased by S, the overall speedup shown in equation (2.4) is:

$$speedup = \frac{1}{(1-f)+\frac{f}{S}} \tag{2.4}$$

An FPGA implementation of a circuit can be viewed as a simulation for hardware of the corresponding digital circuit. Hence results an FPGA-based chip design displays many of the advantages of specialized hardware, including:

i. Parallelism for specific application

ii. Low-power consumption

iii. Valid integration

There are various benefits in reprogrammability:

i. Circuits may be "loaded" as necessary

ii. FPGAs enable the opportunity to upgrade existing installed circuits and significantly cut down time to market.

iii. It is simple to switch to the next-generation production method to take advantage of smaller transistors.

There are many components involved in designing hardware circuits. Few of them are listed here:

i. Combinational logic elements: Basic logic gates are the building blocks of every circuit; by connecting their input and output ports, combinational logic elements can be created that are more intricate.
ii. Memory elements: Sequential logic contains state (memory), whereas combinational logic doesn't contain memory. Practically, sequential logic considered as memory plus combinational logic. The core components of a sequential circuit are elements such as flip-flops, latches, etc., whereas the fundamental component of combinational logic is the logic gate.
iii. Interconnections: connecting to memory and logic components.

Area in FPGAs: The number of slices and 18×18-bit multiplier are used to estimate the size of the FPGA-based hardware (MULT18). The software implementation's area is set to zero because, other from the PowerPC, it uses no extra FPGA resources.

The throughput of the FPGA is calculated using the following equation (2.5):

$$\text{Throughput}=(n*f_{max})/(\text{latency}) \quad (2.5)$$

Where n - amount of input data

f_{max} - maximum input frequency (Hz)

latency - amount of time measured (ns)

Frequency can be calculated using the equation (2.6) and measured in terms of Hertz or cycle per second.

$$f = 1/T = N/t. \quad (2.6)$$

Where N - number of cycles

t – time (ns)

The following formulae (2.7) and (2.8) can be used to generate the normalized values of area and power usage for comparisons, respectively [133].

$$\text{Normalised area} = \frac{\text{Area} \times 10^3}{(\text{Tech.}/90\,\text{nm})^2 \times M \times \log_2 N} \quad (2.7)$$

$$\text{Normalised power} = \frac{\text{Power} \times \text{Execution time} \times 10^3}{V_{DD}^2 \times M \times N \times \log_2 N} \quad (2.8)$$

[133] presents the normalized power calculation. The formulae used to derive the normalized values are shown in (2.9): -

$$\text{Normalised power}_{\text{proposed}} = \frac{\text{Power} \times \text{Execution time} \times 10^2}{V_{DD}^2 \times M \times N} \quad (2.9)$$

where M - number of sorted elements

N - element's width.

2.2 Programming for hardware

Schematics were the sole official means of representing a circuit in the early stages of designing electrical circuits. In the past, options are either draw circuits by hand or with a CAD tool. Utilizing a suitable Hardware Description Language (HDL) is currently the most popular method of designing a circuit.

2.2.1 Hardware Description Languages (HDLs)

The frequently used hardware description languages are Verilog/VHDL (used to programme FPGAs as well). A Hardware Description Language (HDL) primarily resembles a common computer language, such as C. However, there are notable distinctions between a language created to manufacture hardware circuits and one created to generate assembly code for a microprocessor.

HDLs are structured programming languages. It is composed of following ability:

i. Captures the hierarchy of circuit and connection

ii. Practically express the intrinsic parallelism of various chip components

iii. Offers an in built method for software circuit in behaviour simulation

2.2.2 Simulation

Hardware circuit design requires the use of simulation as a vital tool affordably because constructing a hardware circuit is an expensive and time-consuming operation. Because simulation is so essential, supporting methods are already built into the HDL. A circuit can be simulated at several levels of granularity. Verifying a circuit's behavioural correctness is typically done as the first stage in the design process.

In addition, a suitable testbench is constructed in the HDL along with a behavioural model of the circuit. The circuit can then be assessed using a software simulator compared with the test cases listed in the testbench. Next is the design phase, structural components slowly take the place of behavioural part, and the logical correctness, such timing compliance, start to matter.

This kind of simulation is also supported by HDLs; for instance, modules may include annotations like estimated timing data, such as additional delay, etc. A simulator can determine whether a designed circuit can withstand a specific clock frequency.

2.3 Building block of FPGAs

Combinational logic in an ASIC is created by connecting a number of physically simple logic gates. These logic gates are replicated in FPGAs using numerous occurrences of a generic component known as a look-up table, or simply LUT.

i. LUT representation:

   A function with arbitrary Boolean values and up to n Boolean parameters can be implemented using an n-input LUT. Figure 2.1 provides two straightforward illustrations of AND gates and OR gates, both of which are implemented using two-input LUTs.

Input	Output
00	0
01	0
10	0
11	1

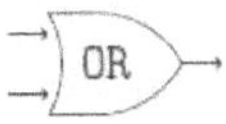

Input	Output
00	0
01	1
10	1
11	1

Figure 2.1: Representation of AND and OR gate of 2-input LUT

ii. Internal Design of a LUT:

An n-input LUT requires 2n bits of SRAM to hold the lookup table and 2n × 1 multiplexers typically implemented as a tree of 2 × 1 multiplexers—to read out a specific configuration bit. The norm used to be 4-input LUTs, however 6-input LUTs are becoming more prevalent. Figure 2.2 provides a 4-input LUT example for readability.

iii. LUTs as memory elements:

LUT consists of SRAM and is an essential part. LUTs can also be considered as memory components in a circuit that uses an FPGA. LUTs can also be set up to function as so-called distributed RAM when an FPGA is designed, i.e., as a tiny LUT consists of n×1 components. Then, it is possible to combine several LUT RAMs for wider and/or deeper memories. When embedded RAM blocks in a circuit are relatively small, such as to create tiny FIFOs, distributed RAM is a useful option. Another important memory component that LUTs can be set to implement is shift registers.

Programmable logic block is considered to be the building blocks of FPGA. The memory requirement of the FPGA is afforded by the fabric and local memory interconnects. In programmable logic blocks, large number of Look Up Table (LUT) components are twined to each other. The LUT is opted to be the building blocks because of its n input and 1 output multiplexer like working capability. A complex programmable logic block can be made by combining multiple LUT's together.

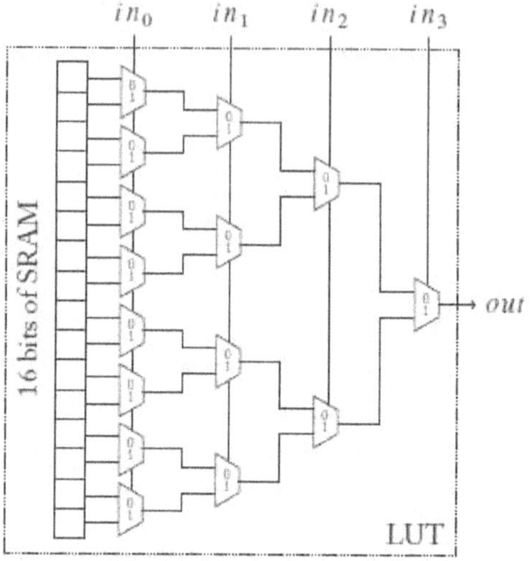

Figure 2.2: 4-input LUT

In addition to the programmable logic circuits available in FPGA, supplementary miniature modules such as registers, flip flops, Random Access Memory (RAM) etc. are also employed to meet the memory resource terms [33], [38], [39]. With the growth attained on embedded domain, recent year FPGA are outfitted with additional resources such as multi core CPU, Digital Signal Blocks, UltraRAM in-memory resource, configurable I/ O blocks etc.

2.4 Layers in FPGA devices

The following are the two separate layers that make up FPGA devices:

i. Configuration memory
ii. Hardware logic

The hardware logic layer mainly consists of the computational hardware resources. This layer includes Digital Signal Processing (DSP) blocks, lookup tables (LUTs), memory blocks, transceivers, flip-flops, and others, are found. Additionally, this layer also has the switch boxes and routing resources needed to connect components to create circuits.

Configuration file/bitstream is a binary file in deployment process. The configuration memory layer utilizes this file for holding FPGA related configuration data. Mainly bitstream file consists of all required initial values. This values related to memories, set-reset flip-flop values, initial value for the input-output pins, voltage standards and related routing information. Thus, the configuration memory values serve as the main determinant of the function that the hardware logic layer will implement.

2.5 Database Management in FPGA

FPGA-based accelerators have showed success in deploying for betterment of high-performance database systems, which are essential to many applications [67]. As databases can readily reach "Big Data" dimensions and take up terabytes of RAM, database systems could be demanding. Online Transaction Processing (OLTP) systems were the majority of database systems in the past. These systems stand out for their straightforward transactional processes. Another database category called On-line Analytical Processing (OLAP), that contains more complex queries that require to retrieve, summarize and analyze multidimensional data, evolved with the development in data mining and machine learning in big data [67]. FPGAs have been seen as an appealing answer in the latter group because many processes access the data in a continuous manner and the queries are occasionally pipelineable.

The synergy between three key principles must be properly taken advantage of in order to fully harness the advantage of FPGA in DBMS:

1. Utilisation of target designs for hardware and software that are scalable and heterogeneous
2. Query subdivision and refinement
3. Reconfiguring hardware on the fly

Due to multi-integration system, it has become meticulous for the system designers to deploy FPGA on any adhoc environment. Management of database plays a significant part in the establishment of FPGA system. There are two distinguished ways for integrating FPGA modules into DBMS: one way is by placing the FPGA on the data source component of the buffer layer service and second way is sharing workload for the given tasks like co-processor scheme [40], [41]. In contrast to the aforementioned connectivity technique, [42] recent years have seen approaches for database connecting via data movement intervals. Such trials resulted in faster database operations, which helped many industrial scale databases accept database operations. An example of such database operation is Baidu's software namely Spark, Hive etc. [43]. This appears the FPGA database acceleration technique in several database systems. It supports operations in abstract SQL.

The domain of analytical databases has seen many advancements along with accelerator-based research. Today's widely used column-oriented databases, like MonetDB [125], typically perform minimum order of magnitude better than row-oriented ones and can efficiently use multi-core CPUs. Due to this, the speedup factor of FPGAs provide for fundamental SQL operators have decreased, and they frequently aren't sufficient to justify the extra work required to include specialist hardware into the server architecture.

In order to advance datacenter capabilities beyond what can be provided by commodity server architectures, a composable reconfigurable fabric was devised and developed [127]. In order to operate FPGAs at scale, Catapult Fabric assesses what problems need to be solved and whether significant performance benefits for demanding production workloads are possible.

The main intention of using acceleration engine like FPGA is to execute database operations efficiently in analytical queries [131]. Without needing any modifications to the application or the current data structure, the suggested method offers a means for a DBMS to easily utilize the FPGA processing capability. The accelerator can be customized to run various queries without reconfiguring itself by creating a query specific control block. This prototype is put into practice in an FPGA system that is PCIe-attached along with incorporated into a dynamic server and commercial DBMS platform [131]. When compared to the cost of the baseline programme and real customer data, the results show up to an absolute faster dump for computations and up to 94% CPU reduction achieved.

FPGA packages are less expensive than other system-specific packages that give designers ample license and resources to develop an accelerator. The database operation expands in response to user demand, making the deployment of a general-purpose database processor costlier. Aside this reasons, FPGA surpasses all IO database processors and ASIC designs [44]. The use of FPGA on the coprocessor level improves database adaptability for any particular applications. Figure 2.3 depicts the layout of the DBMS with various structural layers.

The three specific layer levels are SQL, Data and Buffer service which can be customized in database accelerators [45].

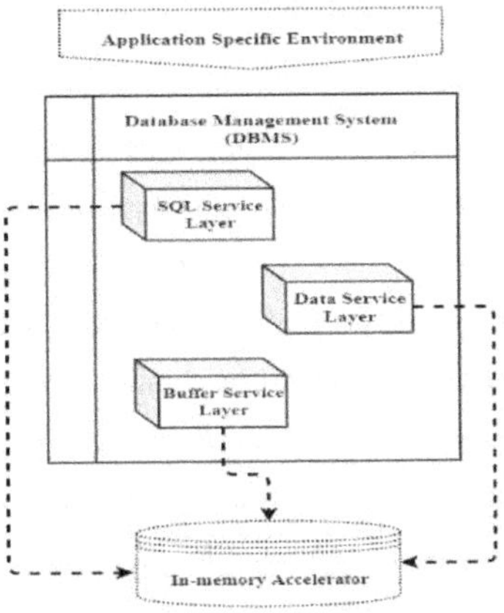

Figure 2.3 Overview of FPGA DBMS Accelerator

An FPGA accelerator handles database related queries using DBMS. The functionality of the service layer is to provide the interfaces, logic management and other services. In the buffer layer, the job requests are queued and SQL layer provides the database operation functionalities. However, the main challenges in database accelerators are throughput and latency [46] [47].

a) Throughput: the data flow inside the system effects the memory bandwidth, as the data flow consumes higher bandwidth results in lower throughput. This logic is also applicable to FPGA accelerator, because of the large demand in accessing data leads to memory inheritance [48] [49].

b) Latency: an unpredictable main memory access leads to latency. The CPU/accelerator should be answerable to the cause of memory latency. One such reason for memory latency is sorting operation carried out in database [45].

Accelerators can be classified into two types:

1. Database accelerators: An energy-efficient query processing and optimization service is offered by a database accelerator. The database accelerators provide two types of frameworks:

   a. Database-specific frameworks: Centaur [44] is a typical piece of task for implementing a combination of hardware and software solution. Continuation to Centaur framework hardware component solution can be named as "FThreads manager" and the software component solution as the "Application interface" [131]. This together make up the entire system [131]. Through MonetDB's UDF (User Defined Function) capabilities, the product allows API calls in C++ [106]. The hardware component is in charge of controlling the various types of hardware required by user in terms of fetching data from memory, resource utilization, and pipelining [131].

      Centaur is extended by DoppioDB [107]. Utilizing the UDF functionality as provided by MonetDB to make calls to the hardware accelerator. DoppioDB leverages MonetDB together with a various hardware designs of optimized FGPA devices. DoppioDB uses FPGA to implement filtering using skyline operators, regular expression, and random data access while leaving the CPU to handle the remaining burden [131].

      Only compute-intensive operators are offloaded to the FPGA using Centaur, maintaining lightweight operators on the CPU. To further boost performance and minimise data transfer between the FPGA and main memory, hardware operators can also be pipelined.

b. General-purpose frameworks: as we know there are number of frameworks which might not be related to databases directly but could be an important part of a comprehensive system for speeding up database operations on FPGAs [131]. An effort to offer virtualization facilities for FPGAs embedded in data centres is one example of a framework that addresses a larger area of applications [108]. The primary work concentrated in this [108] paper is the expansion of the OpenStack framework. The expansion possible by enabling the tools to assign FPGA resources to clients while maintaining performance and usability standards.

   The approach [131] relies mostly on partial reconfiguration. Since the static logic that controls the client programmable Virtualized FPGA Resources (VFRs) is the primary element of the FPGA design [131]. Input and output arbitrators make for quick, secure communication and do away with unpredictable states, which are the key components of static logic.

2. Operator accelerators: hash, join, select, merge, sort, string related operators, and arithmetic are some of the subcategories of database operator accelerators. The data placement element defines the data's initial location at the moment of the request. But the access pattern attribute describes how the patterns of data is moving in database [131].

   a. Sort: this operator can be quite helpful in a database system because various queries involve hashing, aggregations or merging tables. This operation can be considered as most expensive operation depending on implementation and requirements [33]. They [49] showed that an FPGA-based operation uses as far as low power than a processor for equivalent performance and that closer coordination between an FPGA and a CPU can actually improve overall performance.

      It is being examined that heterogeneous merge sort, a practical use-case that executes the final stages of the merging on the CPU for data that does not fill the FPGA memory. They assessed the performance of sorting logic on FPGA (odd-even sort and bitonic sort) [131].

b. Join: Relational databases frequently perform the join operation. [131] Join's primary role is to merge the same attributes of two tables using various norm. Equi-join considered as a popular join operation that merges vertically with similar values in their corresponding columns by performing an equality comparison on the input data from two tables. There are numerous join algorithms with FPGA implementations, including hash join, nested-loop join and sort-merge join.
c. String matching: [131] the best scripts for string matching is regular expressions. This concise scripts with sophisticated capabilities for complex string matching. Non-strictly structured data, like strings, can become the bottleneck in analytical databases with the increase of machine learning and incorporating the relation algebras for analytical processes. [107]
d. Arithmetic: A group of operators connected to machine learning, statistics and big data analytics are additional accelerators provided in improving contemporary database organization [131].

2.6 Sort operator

Any database management system must perform sorting as a fundamental activity. When input tuples are sorted using these operators, a variety of other database operators, including joins and GROUP BY aggregation, find its usage effectively. Sorting, however, is a somewhat intensive operation that can end up being a query plan's bottleneck. Therefore, speeding up sorting can significantly improve a database's total query processing performance.

The main responsibility of the query optimizer implementation is to choose suitable and cost effective approach. Authors in [119] suggested employing partial reconfiguration for sort operations. This technique proposed to change the resource allocation of a tree-based merge sorter and FIFO-based merge sorter in accordance with the complexity of the challenge.

[128] utilizes the FPGAs' inherently parallel BRAMs topology to speed up the BST search. By comparing several strategies, the utility of this technology is illustrated using various trade-offs on latency, throughput, and resource usages, including tree duplication and partitioning.

2.6.1 Sorting Networks

The main intention is to stream unsorted data to sorted data in sorting networks. This can be achieved via a sequences of compare-and-swap elements. Then data will be sorted in the desired order as a result. However, at these fast processing rates, moving data into and out of the FPGA soon becomes challenging. As additional inputs are added, the sorting circuits complexity increases exponentially. Consequently, this sorting networks are efficient and suitable only for small data set values at a given instance. It is remarkably efficient to develop a sort instruction on hardware-accelerated microprocessor for sorting SIMD registers.

There is various way to represent Compare-And-Swap (CAS) units. They are as follows:

a. Conventional CAS: The compare-and-swap element is made up of two cross-coupled 32-bit multiplexers that are driven by a 32-bit comparator [104]. Input B and Input A will be switched if the Input B is lesser than that of A and this will be chosen by both multiplexers. Figure 2.4 represents the basic compare-and-swap (CAS) unit.

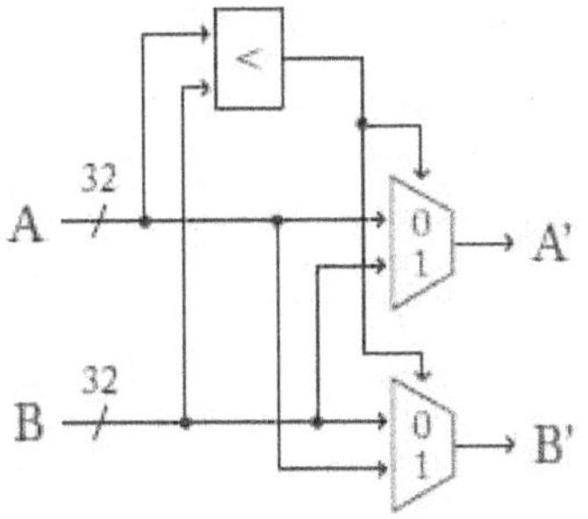

Figure 2.4: Basic Compare-and-Swap (CAS) Unit

b. Compare-and-Select Unit: If it is possible to offload larger chunks of data to the FPGA for complete sorting, by doing so communication between the CPU and FPGA would be reduced, giving the CPU more time to manage other tasks while the FPGA sorts. An alternative is to create a merge sorter that uses BRAM-based FIFO queues to effectively sort bigger problem magnitudes in the FPGA. Figure 2.5 represents the basic compare-and-select unit.

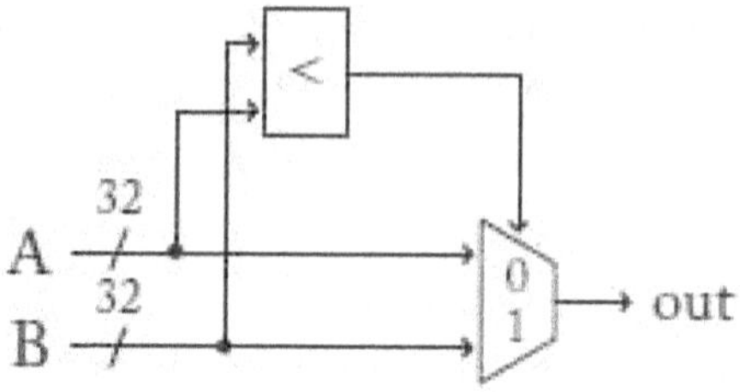

Figure 2.5: Compare-and-Select Unit

The compare-and-swap unit from the aforementioned section is split in half by the select-value component, which compares two values A and B and selects the minimum of the two. A larger sorted run can be created by combining two smaller sorted runs using the select-value component.

c. CAS in unary design: The maximum/minimum operations on the set of elements are the basic functions of CAS blocks. Because of this, hardware CAS block and sorting network implementation is a perfect fit for unary processing [55]. Figure 2.6 represents CAS in unary design consisting of one AND gate and OR gate. This circuit also gives the minimum and maximum value of two inputs as depicted in figure.

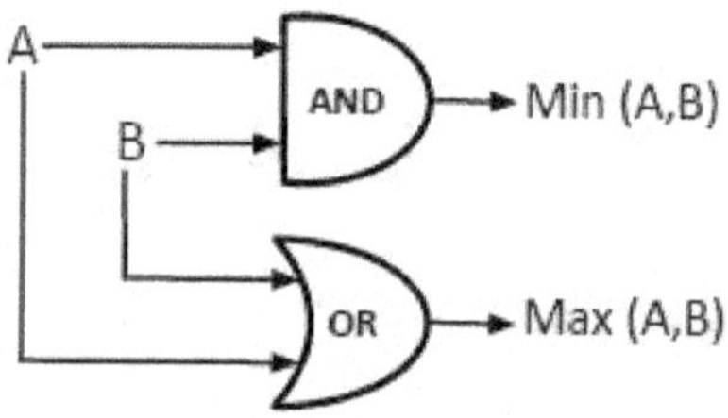

Figure 2.6: CAS in unary design

The CAS block can be created with just one AND and one OR gate. This CAS block does not depend on the complex logic. Therefore, regardless of the input data's resolution, the sorting logic can be synthesized. Although the synthesized circuit will be considerably less expensive than the circuit synthesized using the binary approach. But there is additional overhead which must be incurred for conversion units that are required to convert the data between the binary and the unary format. The time spent is a lengthier operation on 2M-bit long streams.

2.7 Hardware-Software Co-design

Hardware/Software co-design is one of the efficient way of design suggested in [120]. The FPGA accelerator can also be suitable for pipeline with feedforward design. This hardware kernels includes selection, sorting and projection operation. Query can be accelerated considering parameters like run-time and time required for tuple processing. In CPU-based host system, pre-processing of data is one of the acceleration technique. Hence later the data can be carried out for further processing. In this work, its proved that combining hardware and software results better.

The hardware has a limit on how quickly data management and analysis systems can execute queries and retrieve data. This hardware/software co-design is about optimizing algorithm and its data structures. The hardware performance requirements for both older/compute-intensive applications. They are more suitable for contemporary data-intensive applications. This includes parameters like bandwidth, capacity, and access latency. The comparison made by considering standard benchmarks which is cost-effective and energy efficient. Under this varied application needs, the conventional data management and analysis approaches are encountering completely unforeseen obstacles [121].

2.8 Merge Sorter

The sorting logic suitable for huge data elements is Merge sort [101] and bubble sort works best for a small data set. Because merge sort cannot keep elements in RAM and is ideal for huge data sets, it develops a hybrid sort-merge strategy. External sorting is another name for it. Merge parallel sorting is supported by FPGA.

In [101], on the basis of resource utilization, delay, clock cycles, power, and area comparisons are done between various sorters like serial-merge sort, parallel-merge sort, Bitonic-merge sort and odd-even merge sort. Hence, merge unit is an important functional unit in hardware sorting. This merge unit consists of two-input First In First Out (FIFO), 1-output FIFO, comparator and a multiplexer. The two input FIFOs contains a sorted data set that requires a merging operation to output sorted FIFO.

The Table 2.1 reports the complete details of FIFO based merge sorter approach by describing advantages, disadvantages and future scope of each approach.

2.9 Low Power Sorter Design Trade-offs

Hardware acceleration is frequently used to improve performance and to fulfil the need for real-time processing. High-speed processing, however, typically results in significantly increased power consumption. To fix this problem, [51] provides hardware architecture with a low-power and high-throughput model. This modular hardware architecture suitable for a partial sorting network. The comparing modules use a pointer-like design to change sample indexes rather than the input data itself. By reducing switching activity and signal transitions, power consumption is decreased. An iterative architecture is suggested that makes use of both a new clipping technique and a low-power sorting module to avoid the needless comparison of the enormous data set.

The typical method involves setting up a batcher (or bitonic) network, which is a logic of compare-and-swap devices. Pipelining such networks is a simple process. This [55] suggests a novel "unary processing"-based technique to sorting networks that is both space- and power-efficient. The numbers are uniformly encoded as a stream of 0s and 1s in unary processing. The values are determined by the proportion of 1s in the stream, followed by a sequence of one value (let's say 1) and a sequence of the other value (let's say 0). Complete sorting networks' synthesis results indicate up to a 92% area and power saving over traditional binary implementations. But this method increases latency.

These sorting units are frequently designed utilizing top-of-the-line FPGA circuits to enable the capability and adaptability needed for high-energy physics research.

Table 2.1 An survey of Merge sorter using FIFO technique

Merge sorter using FIFO	Advantages	Remarks
Baseline approach- uses 2 input FIFO and 1 output FIFO [19]. Time Complexity is O(n) Assumption: two input FIFO elements sorted before.	Every clock cycle a new item is sorted from data set. This iterative process repeated until all the elements sorted.	Inefficient and different strategies can be used Future work: more than 2-input FIFOs can be used and as well increase the levels of FIFO.
Circulating merge sorter approach- uses two FIFO, one is input FIFO and other one to accumulate sorted data [109]. Time Complexity is $O(n^2)$	Easily scalable to handle different size data sets. Speedup achieved compared to quick sort software approach Easily adaptable to different data types.	Can be enhanced to Pipelined based FIFO merge sorting, parallel hardware merge sorting.
Cascading Merge sorter using FIFO - multiple Merge sorter using FIFO in cascaded fashion [110]	Useful for generating longer fully sorted sequence	Not suitable for continuous streaming of data
FIFO based merge sorter tree-structured architecture for largescale sorting [111]. Time Complexity is $O(N\log_K N)$ – conventional method, proposed method- O(K) for K input leaves	Achieves high performance	Results in high hardware overhead
Parallel Merge Tree(PMT) sorter- consist of mergers of 2 lists and FIFO queues. Time complexity is O(n) [112]	Provides high throughput	Not scalable for high number of inputs
Hybrid Parallel Merge Tree (HPMT)- Large utility sorters, Time complexity is $O(\log_2(k))$ [113]	Performance required throughput. many-leaf merges at the same time with minimal hardware resources	BRAM is not suitable, DRAM is best suitable
Wide Merge Sorter (WMS) – Dequeue Architecture [114]	In the VMS merge network, replace the two (E, E) merges with a single (2E, E) merger. First, within the merge network, WMS only utilizes one (2E, E) merger. Second, the shift register is not required. Third, the output sorted records in WMS have a lower latency than those in VMS [116].	Consumes more hardware devices
VMS- Very Massive Hardware Merge Sorter [115]	This merge network combines two pipelined mergers.	Higher latency
FLiMS- a Fast Lightweight 2-way Merger for Sorting [117]	Reduced number of hardware resources and achieves high throughput	Limited to fixed width values

Sorting architectures [56] make use of modular design strategies to assemble big sorting units from smaller ones in a hierarchical fashion. Optimized sorting units should select Y largest values from X data elements. This situation usually we face in applications like data mining and analytics, digital signal processing, scientific computing and high power physics.

[93] suggests a brand-new multidimensional sorting algorithm uses 3-D hardware. This sorter unit provides ultralow-power three-dimensional hardware sorting architecture, the so-called Ultralow-Power (ULP). In comparison to earlier methods, the ULP-Sorter architecture dramatically reduces hardware resources and energy consumption. In comparison to earlier survey procedures, the results obtained from simulation reveal that ULP-Sorter reduces the resources in terms of look-up tables and registers. When compared to earlier review, ULP-Sorter averages a 48.7% reduction in the energy consumption of the FPGA. According to this findings, ULP-Sorter is a good design for edge computing devices with space and power restrictions.

Nearly 25% of all computer cycles were dedicated to sorting. As a result, numerous sorting algorithms and their implementations as well as sorting benchmarks were developed. However, those benchmarks do not adequately take into account the growing heterogeneity in the form of the data, nor do they evaluate the architectural aspects of various computer systems based on the algorithmic choice. In order to address these problems and aid in the assessment of sorting algorithms from both a software- and hardware-perspective, this [94] work suggests the creation of a thorough sorting benchmark framework.

Real-Time Hardware Sorter (RTHS) is an innovative hardware-based multidimensional sorting method presented in [132]. This approach more suitable for new applications intending for huge data processing where resources and performance are main concerns. RTHS main idea is to use sorting technique that results in high-performance and scalable. Due to this hardware features, a well-designed parallel hardware sorting architectures (PHSAs) used in applications. The suggested approach can also be utilized in big data applications to construct Min/Max queues or identify the biggest/smallest entries. This approach reduced the hardware resources in terms of lookup tables. Also provides better results compared to the other sorting logic. The implementation was carried out on a Virtex-7 FPGA.

2.10 Benefits of Comparison-free Sorting

[54] present a new sorting method known as comparison-free sorting, which instantly sorts the integer elements of input data without comparing them to any other data. This hardware-based sorting algorithm does not require processor memory or complicated circuitry. It uses simple logic and straight forward registers to store and process the data. Then performs the matrix-mapping operation and results in sorted sequence of elements. As a result, the complexity of the entire transistor count is the order of O(N).

[57] proposed sorting algorithm model that uses comparison-free sorting to arrange data components without using data comparisons. The hardware-based sorting method uses the Hamming memory and SRAM-based memory structure to store the components according to their Hamming maximum order representations. For N data items it takes 2N clock cycles, the outputted sorted items are produced using a straightforward matrix multiplication. This results obtained by using the buffer and the Hamming memory. Binary equivalent of data items is also saved in a serial fashion shift buffer.

The basic OR and AND gates are utilized in the NCL unit to design a sorting unit component. The sorting unit proposed a free of comparison as an improvement over the NCL unit [58]. In Comparison-free unit, data are not subject to comparison operations involving the maximum and minimum terms associated with AND-OR gates. For the purpose of performing the sorting unit, comparison-free units generally use matrix-mapping operations with one-hot matrices and binary matrices. Results of sorting i.e. comparison-free on the verification of power, transistor count per area, and timing unit. Contrasting comparison-free sorting to null convention sorting results in a significant reduction in power, space, and time.

This study [60] introduces a hardware-based free of comparison sorting logic that sorts P numbers of components entirely in P iterations. The first iteration of the proposed architecture is successful in locating the largest element [60]. The following largest element is then determined from the remaining data items in each subsequent iteration. The structure accepts elements from an unsorted array, finds the largest element every clock cycle, and then stores the data elements in a Sorted Memory (SM) unit. The sort controller is in charge of overall controlling, including initiating the clock and transmitting the appropriate control signals to the appropriate units.

The sorting method used in DAS [61] is essentially a combination of the counting sort algorithm and the radix-2 sort algorithm. In other words, the input data are sorted bit-by-bit using the counting sort algorithm. Usually starts from the MSB (most significant bit) and ends at LSB (least significant bit). Important features of DAS are that it regenerates input data in sorted order as opposed to exchanging or moving it to another location in memory. DAS can sort N of k-bit binary data using just N k bit of memory. DAS has hardware complexity of $O(N^2)$. Even if N^2 sorting cells are needed, the sorting cell's simplicity lessens the hardware overhead. Just enough space is needed in memory for DAS to hold the sorted data. Its little memory need and straightforward sorting-cell structure make DAS a scalable design.

For negative and positive items, a comparison-free sorting method that meet requirements like hardware complexity is proposed [62]. The main goal is to arrange the array of input elements without comparing any data elements of a given array. Similar technology is used for the sorting of negative and positive numbers. As a result, no complicated hardware design is needed. This prevents the use of any circuitry with a complex design, such as those used in other traditional sorting methods, or any memory, such as SRAM. Instead, the suggested method stores the binary elements in simple registers. In order to minimize hardware complexity, a comparison-free sorting algorithm is developed for the FSM module. ModelSim SE10.4d simulator is used to verify each design after it has been coded in VHDL. Synopsys DC Design Compiler and Vivado are used to synthesize both conventional and proposed designs (90 nm CMOS technology) [62]. The author introduced comparison-free sorting algorithm using finite state machine and also proved this approach consumes less power and space than the standard chip, according to the synthesis report.

In this work [97], researchers proposed a hardware sorting methodology which is free of comparison. In this algorithm, M data elements takes M clock cycles. Also identifies the largest element in the very first clock cycle. Each block in this design consist of basic logic gates. Such M blocks are arranged in cascaded form to build a sorting engine. Sorting and storing actions are performed in a pipelined stage of this architecture. For multiple data sets, the entire design is synthesized, starting with pseudo randomly created data elements and continuing through unique elements, identical elements, and also random to entirely sorted data elements. The order of the input elements does not effect this hardware sorter. The synthesis results also showed that this method uses a fair amount of FPGA resources.

2.11 Sorters and softcore processors in RISC-V

Hardware-based methods that take advantage of parallelism include sorting networks, systolic sorters, and linear sorters. Designed with identical nodes and simple control, linear sorters offer lower latency and area requirements than sorting networks but have a lower throughput. [70] describes a system that uses several simultaneous acting linear sorters to boost throughput.

The demand of the application keeps varying. Also depends on the factors like pipeline depth and memory interleaving. The main purpose of interleaving is to boost the bandwidth and permits to sort multiple values in a clock cycle. [70] speedup achieved by the factor of 68 implemented on FPGA and MicroBlaze soft core processor.

However, the high power consumption, large device size, and poor performance of FPGA-based designs prevent them from being widely used in low-power embedded systems using soft-core processors. In this research [73], describes an effective reconfigurable architecture and construction of soft-core processors in SRAM-based FPGAs. This design taken care of less utilization of resources and fragmented accessibility of the designed units. To do this, merge the underutilized functional units into effectively created Reconfigurable Units (RUs) based on look-up tables (LUTs). In this work, to further boost the effectiveness of the recommended design, a set of effective customizable hard logics were employed. But actual implementation based on the occurrence of Boolean functions and LUTs.

Additionally, [73] tested the Berkeley RISC-V processor implementation. Authors also proposed architecture using MiBench benchmarks. Evaluated the viability of the suggested architecture on a digital signal processing core and a different open-source CPU (LEON2). This work was compared with the existing soft-core processors based on LUT design. [73] shows the improvement in terms of power, area, and execution time.

Soft-core processors are gaining popularity as an alternative for embedded system architectures because of the flexibility they provide. Reconfigurable computing devices versatility gives designer the chance to quickly identify the optimum design trade-offs and accomplish certain application goals. The SecretBlaze is designed to provide highly configurable and open-source RISC soft-core processor that is presented in this work [74]. This model is emphasized for its modular approach, which tries to compromise between the data path efficiency and the quality of the design. The SecretBlaze is an extremely promising processor, as shown by results from synthesis and performance tests.

Using layered domain-specific hardware languages and highly parameterized generators, the new hardware language Chisel offers advanced hardware design [75]. By including concepts like object oriented concepts, functional programming, parameterized types, and type inference into Chisel, which is built on top of the Scala programming language, raises the standard for hardware design abstraction. For translating synthesis of FPGA/ASIC flow, a C++ software simulators or Verilog code is used in Chisel Model. Benefits of utilizing Scala language are supports feature like those for developing circuit generators, being domain-specific languages, compiling to the JVM, having development tools and IDEs, and having a substantial and expanding user base. With the above features, Scala can be considered as very strong language.

The reconfigurable computing system MorphoSys is proposed in this work [77] to investigate the viability of employing processors for word-level and computationally high intensive applications. This model processor is an integrated, reconfigurable, coarse-grained system-on-chip that is made for high-throughput and data-parallel applications. The architecture is made up of an efficient memory interface unit, a modified RISC CPU core, and processing cells which has reconfigurable capability. The reconfigurable processor array, control processor, data and configuration memories, and other components of the MorphoSys architecture are discussed in this work.

There has been an increase in the variety of workloads for computing devices as a result of the development of highly specialized embedded computer systems. The varied requirements of these applications are difficult for general-purpose processors to successfully handle, and specialized hardware is rarely an option. The authors claim that reconfigurable computing, combines the adaptability of general-purpose processors with the efficiency of specialized hardware devices, provides the key to a solution. The new architecture for reconfigurable computing developed by the authors consists of PipeRench [78] and its companion compiler. PipeRench handles a system's diverse computing needs without requiring unique hardware device. Logic granularity, configuration time, forward compatibility, hard limitations, and compilation time are just a few of the issues with FPGA architectures that the authors discuss in their description of the PipeRench architecture.

The best solution to enhance the performance of application-specific procedures is usage of reconfigurable hardware devices in an application. Chimaera, introduced in [79] incorporates many powerful features. This prototype includes compact reconfigurable unit inside pipeline stages and like superscalar processor provides facility to dynamically schedule the queries. On integer data, Chimaera is possible to do out operations with nine inputs and one output. In this article, details about the Chimaera incorporated C compiler, which quickly map the computations in Reconfigurable Functional Unit (RFU) for execution.

Chimaera can perform the following tasks:

1. Compress all instructions into RFU for operations
2. Transform control-flow instructions into RFU for further operations
3. This prototype supports fine grain data parallelism and instructions for multimedia extension suitable for integer operations

By comparing Application Specific Integrated Circuit (ASIC) equivalent, Look-Up Tables (LUTs) suffer from severe performance and space overheads due to their extensive flexibility in performing arbitrary operations. Utilizing less flexible logic pieces that can implement the majority of logic functions is one way to reduce such overheads.

In this study [80], first examined the most popular benchmark functions, then developed a collection of low flexible but more effective logic cells, known as Hard Logics (HL). Given the variety of classes that higher input functions fall under; so suitable decomposition used to divide them into smaller size groups. This groups further simplified the HL design or produce low input functions. To achieve maximum logic resource consumption, [80] used a heterogeneous LUT-HL architecture and a mapping mechanism are also suggested.

The possibility has emerged to revive the study of CPU microarchitecture thanks to the open RISC-V ISA. Using a straightforward fork-join structure in the execute stage, [82] suggested a multi-cycle execution unit of RVCoreP. This work also supports M-extension with the least amount of overhead. This approach can be used to increase the support for both custom instructions and other extensions included in RISC-V.

Compared to the in-order 5-stage pipeline architecture benchmark programmes from Dhrystone, Coremark, and Embench to RV32IM and RV32I, it is found that RV32IM performed on average better than RV32I. The M-extension of RV32I has responsibility to design the remainder, division and multiplication instruction as per system requirement. And discovered that RV32IM uses about 1.5 times as many FPGA resources as RV32I does. The softcore processor performs the iterative multipliers like the radix-4 booth multiplier.

In this work [83], Alibaba T-Head division introduces the Xuantie-910 a top-tier integrated 64-bit RISC-V microprocessor with outstanding performance. This system is entirely based on the RV64GCV instruction set and offers specialized additions to arithmetic and logic instructions, bit manipulation instructions, load-store instructions, Translation lookaside buffer and cache related operations. For high efficiency vector processing, it also implements the RISCV vector extension standard 0.7.1 stable version.

Xuantie-910 supports Multi-core, multi-cluster SMP with cache coherence functionality. Recent applications expect the feature of the vector extension and custom extensions. The toolchain present in the processor has been greatly improved. The best performance is currently provided by the Xuantie-910 through co-optimization of the hardware and toolchain (in terms of instruction count, number of clock cycles, speed, and power efficiency).

This study [84] covers the microarchitecture chip design and performs analysis of instruction set supported by RISC-V. The instruction set for the processors are decided during design time and chips are protected by IP rights. The standard companies like Intel, AMD, MIPS and other manufactures also follow the same. Very few processors support open-source ISAs like RISC, SPARC, RISC-V and so on. The University of California, Berkeley's work led to the development of the RISC-V ISA, which was then made available under a BSD license. This work describes the microarchitecture design, analysis, and implications of an instruction set on the pipeline/chip design of a five-stage pipelined RISC-V architecture.

In this study [85], investigated how various microprocessor employs the same ISA execute user-level applications in response to radiation-induced soft errors. Mainly focus on dual processor cores that have different micro-architectural implementations but share the same RISC-V ISA (for in-order/out-of-order). The strong link connected between two CPU processors provide easy fault injection. The processor cores with various ISAs do not exhibit this significant correlation characteristic. Based on this finding, explores a smaller set of fault injection experiments with fewer benchmark applications. This can be used to estimate the impacts of soft threats on a tested processor core.

This paper [87] suggests a change to the RISC pipelined processors architecture that gets rid of the penalty for execution time caused by code instrumentation in this model. The author introduced non-intrusive tracing and also examined the sequence and execution time of program after adding traces. This technique built on RISC-V processor created using VHDL as a case study. A collection of instrumented code examples produced using a worst-case execution time estimation tool were executed and evaluated on the CPU, which was synthesized on an FPGA. The outcomes demonstrate that the suggested architecture efficiently runs the instrumented code.

Authors [88] chose to tightly integrate an eFPGA into the CPU instruction area as strategy. Compared to other techniques, this requires less interface logic. Because unique instructions sometimes employ FPGA fabrics with only a few thousands or hundreds of thousands of LUTs, the price of an interface could quickly rise to the level of a significant cost component. Using a serial external programming interface, direct loading of the compiled custom instruction configuration bit-streams into the eFPGA fabric is possible. As an alternative, this technique is offering a special instruction that allows the CPU to self-configure the eFPGA while running programmes (accessible through a C API).

[89] suggested the RSD processor. This processor model incorporates open-source, FPGA-optimized RISC-V softcore processor. Speculative scheduling, Out-of-Order memory related instruction, execution and disambiguation, a dependence predictor, and a nonblocking cache memory are just a few of the aggressive OoO execution capabilities that the RSD enables. The RSD uses FPGA characteristics while also supporting such demanding features. As a result, it uses less FPGA resources than the current OoO soft processors, which struggle to accommodate such aggressive features. This work presents the final product of the RSD microarchitecture design before outlining many cutting-edge optimization methods.

SecretBlaze [91] is based on the MicroBlaze instruction set and also an open-source soft-core processor introduced. It is quite flexible, balanced processing efficiency and space cost to satisfy the needs of embedded chip design. The SecretBlaze is a research tool and also suitable for use in economical systems. Although it was initially created to research cryptographic protections, its modular design increases the chances for reuse in several research and teaching endeavors.

2.12 Research Gaps

The present research of sorting algorithms on FPGA/ASIC components are based on algorithms which are possible to implement in hardware and High Performance in hardware implementation. The architecture of hardware sorting units varies depending on the desired applications. Also depends on the input numbers and the size. The majority of the sorting methods that have been recently proposed mainly aim to increase computational effectiveness.

According to a literature review, the main obstacles to construct large sorting networks include:

1. The biggest problem faced is lengthy critical paths. As the input bit width grows, critical path also increases.

   - Hence overall performance is decreased by the long critical pathways' impact on operating frequency.

   - Sorters implemented in a pipeline will perhaps lessen the critical paths.

2. Implementing pipelines dramatically that increases switching activity between stages and makes the design more power-hungry.

   - The increased power hunger can be reduced by implementing the appropriate low-power strategies.

The three research gaps found from literature survey as follows:

1. A low power sorter architecture must be designed utilizing any structured low power techniques such as DVFS, Power Gating, Multi-Vth and Clock Gating.
2. Designing High Performance Sorters using Low Power circuit/Architectures and Comparison-Free Sorting Architectures.
3. Also to design a customized instruction set for sorting applications in RISC-V microprocessor.

Chapter 3

Low Power Sorters

In a database processor, sorting module can be quite helpful because many queries do aggregations or table merges depending on how they are implemented. Power gating, Clock gating and Dynamic Voltage and Frequency Scaling (DVFS) are few of the widely known low power techniques used during designing chip. In this chapter, the main focus on Low Power Sorters using structured low power techniques.

This chapter consists of: Definition of conventional sorters and its complexity, Literature survey of Low Power Sorters describing technique and implementation methodology, a novel clock gating on conventional sorters and result analysis comparing area, dynamic power and critical path of proposed and conventional sorters and finally, implementation and result analysis of the modified CAS unit and applying Multi -Vth structured low power technique in designing the low power sorters.

3.1 Conventional sorters and its complexity

Sorting is a basic operation in SQL queries. There are many sorting algorithms available and already used by certain applications. In recent decades, sorting is the attracted operations by researchers [50]. Table 3.1 reports the computational complexity of familiar sorting logic.

Table 3.1 Algorithms and Complexity

Sorter Techniques	Best case	Worst case
Bubble sort	O(n)	$O(n^2)$
Quick sort	O(n)	$O(n^2)$
Merge sort	O(nlogn)	O(nlogn)
Insertion sort	O(n)	$O(n^2)$
Heap sort	O(nlogn)	O(nlogn)
Selection sort	$O(n^2)$	$O(n^2)$

From a review of the literature, it is known that odd-even merge sorting and Bitonic sorting are the fastest sorting methods [21] [22] [24]. The hardware sorting units effect the performance and it is a critical parameter. In last few decades, primary concern was on reducing latency and increasing throughput. In any sorting network, the data elements are dependent step by step starting from s0, s1, s2....sn-1 for n items which is carried out in sequential manner. There is an option for the sorters to implement using pure combinational circuits or sequential circuits.

Circuits operated at any step 'k' in pure combinational sorters require the result of step 'k-1' [63]. For a same amount of propagation delay at every stage of the sorter, the total delay of such a combinational sorter will be 'N'. The delay of a clocked sorter is calculated by counting the number of clock cycles required to obtain the final result. The best practice in sequential sorters is pipelining and parallel processing.

3.1.1 Combinational and Sequential Sorters

Combinational circuits are described as being independent of past inputs in terms of producing any output and being time independent. Sequential circuits use both the current and previous inputs to generate output. These circuits are time-dependent.

Advantages of using combinational circuits in designing sorter are:

1. Only the current input is used to determine this output.
2. Quick in execution.
3. It is made to be simple.
4. No feedback exists between the input and the output.
5. This doesn't depend on time.
6. Basic construction blocks: Logic devices
7. Used for Boolean operations and arithmetic.
8. There is no state-storage capacity in combinational circuits.
9. Combinational circuits don't need triggering because they lack a clock.
10. There is no memory component in these circuits.

11. It is simple to handle and use.

Whereas sequential circuits are slow, not easy to design and handle.

One of the concern in combinational sorter implementation is as the data size increases the requirement of hardware resources like LUTs, Slices, Multiplexers etc. also increases enormously. Bitonic sorter and Odd-Even merge sorter is commonly used to handle large random data sets [51] [56]. The constraint on the hardware resources cannot be solved either using ASIC or FPGA.

Generally, Sequential logic implementation of the sorters reduce the hardware components but proportionally there is a rise in the number of clock cycles that can be reduced by pipelining or parallel processing.

3.1.2 Sorting Techniques

The three conventional hardware sorting techniques are Bubble sort, Bitonic sort and Odd-Even sort. In this sorting technique, the implementation of sorters includes a series of compare and swap units as shown in figure 3.1.

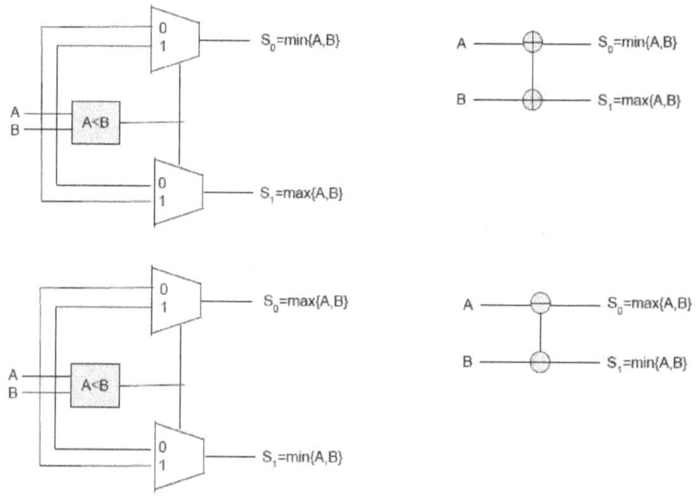

Figure. 3.1: Notation of compare and swap units used in conventional sorters

Given any two values are compared using a comparator as depicted in Figure 3.1. The results drawn at multiplexers generates a sequence in ascending or descending order through selection line of multiplexers. The two conventional symbols + and – represents the ascending/descending order in CAS blocks respectively.

The three conventional sorters are explained as follows:

1. Bubble sort: this sorter suitable for small set of data in hardware. At each round, largest or smallest number is chosen through sequences of comparison units. The run time complexity is $O(M^2)$ for M input size. The bubble sorting philosophy with a series of comparison unit using pipelining is shown in Figure 3.2.

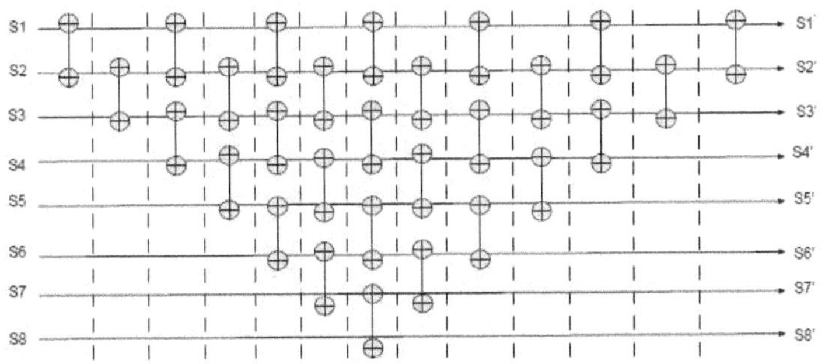

Figure 3.2: Bubble Sorter

2. Odd-Even sort: the sorting process is carried by merging two sorted sequences into a single completed sorted result. Convention used in this technique is OE-M indicating 'M' input odd-even merging unit. The odd-even sorting network is illustrated in Figure 3.3.
3. Bitonic sort: this sorter carried out as a mixture of increasing and decreasing order for the sequence of inputs, which can be merged using merge unit to get the sorted data and convention used in this sorting technique is BM-M for M input size. Figure 3.4 shows the network representation using in Bitonic sorter.

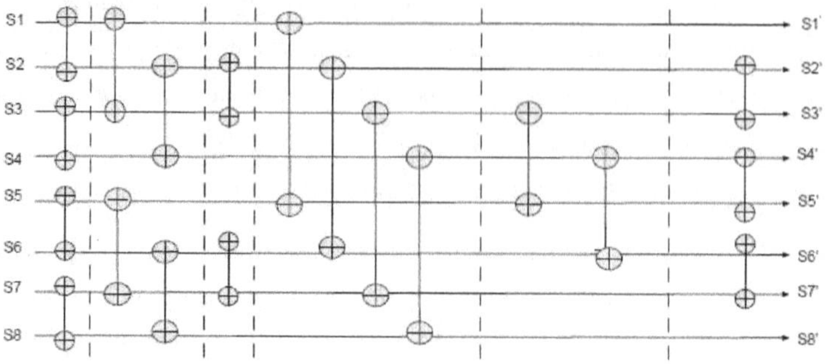

Figure 3.3: Odd-Even Sorter Logic

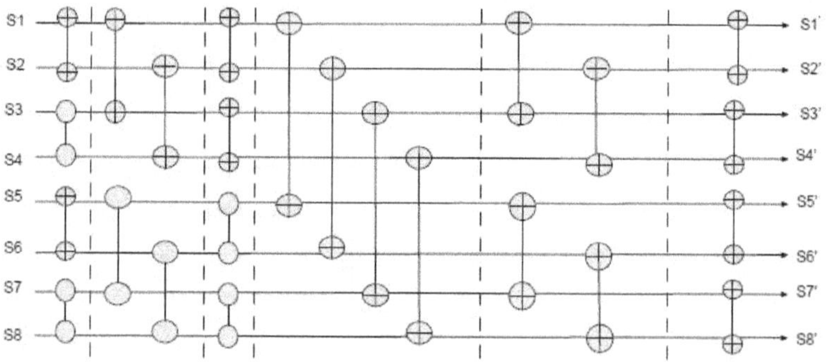

Figure 3.4: Bitonic Sorter

3.1.3 Earlier ASIC implementation vs Modular ASIC techniques of Sorting Algorithms

Application Specific Integrated Circuits (ASIC) that have been specifically designed for a particular application as compared to being made for general use. Large building components like ROM, RAM, EEPROM, flash memory, and other large building blocks are frequently found in modern ASICs, along with microprocessors. A SoC is a common name for such an ASIC (system-on-chip). A Verilog/VHDL, is frequently used by designers of digital ASICs to define the functioning of ASICs. Applications for ASIC include environmental monitoring, personal digital assistants, and auto emission control.

The older ASIC implementations for odd-even sorting algorithm demonstrated in [50]. The authors suggested implementation of this sorting at transistor level with both parallel and serial comparators. The complexity with respect to area and time of sorting algorithm is investigated using a more recent technology of VLSI processing. This model has less restrictions over the I/O chip than preceding generations. The work [50] does fair comparison between pipelined and non-pipelined designs by considering the parameters like area, time and performance.

In [22], discusses the sorting implementation in ASIC by analyzing the parameters like area, timing and memory requirements. The area performance of this architecture is superior for larger numbers, and it is much faster than the fastest hardware sorting engine that has been reported.

Another interesting ASIC implementation is a binary sorting algorithm. This sorting method uses full customized technique. The computational complexity of the sorter is proved to be (n + k -1), where 'n' is the number of k-bit items. Additional improvements to [52] are proposed in [50], making customized hardware implementation consuming relatively less area for huge datasets by putting a reasonable burden on latency. The earlier techniques customized at transistor level which is not suitable for large sorting networks. Hence a modular design techniques required starting from smaller building blocks to design large sorting networks.

The modular approach adopts pipelining and low power [51] [56]. In CMOS designs, dynamic power consumption accounts for the majority of power usage. The dynamic power consumption can be lowered by reducing switching activity. When the number of input data elements increases, switching activity increases. The compare and swap activity in a sorting logic increases switching activity dramatically as bit width grows, resulting in increased dynamic power consumption [53].

[51] proposes an immobile comparison unit that moves sample indexes instead of moving the input data set to reduce dynamic power, and this strategy greatly reduces power. [54] presents a different type of modular technique, in which data is sorted on the fly without any comparison operations. The amount of clock cycles consumed is linearly proportional to the number of inputs, with a speed complexity of order O(N).

In compared to conventional Bitonic sorting networks, the authors of [55] show that unary processing-based Bitonic sorting networks minimize hardware costs and energy usage. Table 3.2 presents comparison of the mentioned low-power techniques.

From literature survey, few of the challenges drawn while designing a large sorting networks are as follows: -

1. Critical path length is the most significant problem identified from survey. This path grows as the input bit width increases. Critical routes with lengthy path reduces operating frequency and overall performance. Sorters that are implemented in a pipeline will reduce critical routes to some extent [56].
2. The pipelined approach considerably increases switching activity and results in high power consumption. Low-power approaches must be used to reduce power usage.

In the existing sorting techniques, low-power approaches like clock gating are not used on hardware implementation in the current sorting logic. As well trade-off between power and performance is not considered.

3.2 Proposed Novel Clock Gated Low Power Sorters

3.2.1 Clock Gating

In most architectures, data is moved into registers only occasionally, whereas the clock signal is constantly provided. At each defined cycle, the clock signal will toggle constantly. The primary source of power dissipation during switching activity is clock signal. The enormous load is driven by the clock signal. The clock is reduced by using a set of flip-flops in the design that are enabled by the control unit. When the register is turned off using the gating function, power is not dissipated during this idle period.

There are various techniques to reduce Dynamic power consumption like reducing clock speed, reduced voltages or cut down the design activity. Clock gating network structure saves the dynamic power consumption required by circuit.

Table 3.2 Brief low power literature survey on Sorting Techniques

Approach	Technology and its implementation	Discussion
Modular Sorter: This sorting units are designed for instances when just the Y largest numbers from a set of X inputs need to be sorted. To meet the requirement, traditional sorting approaches are changed [56].	The 65nm standard cell library is used to synthesize the proposed design. For various input setups, an area and timing analysis report is shown. (Design is semi-custom.)	The proposed sorting network has no power analysis report.
Low power sorter: This paper describes an idea in [56] to reduce power consumption. By adopting a pointers in design, which sample indexes are moved instead of input data, the modular sorting network's dynamic power is diminished [51].	The 90nm standard cell library is used to synthesize the proposed design. For various input configurations, analysis reported for dynamic power and compared to an earlier technique [56]. For various input setups, an area and timing analysis report also presented. (Semi-custom design)	The benefits in power analysis reported in this work. As the bit size of the input increases, and improved power reduction are only seen by decreasing operating frequencies at larger bit-sizes.
Comparison-Free Sorter: this sorting method is presented and implemented which sorts input data integer elements on the fly without comparison [54]. This technique has a complexity of O(N), which is a substantial contribution.	The 90nm standard cell library is used to synthesize the proposed design. The power results, transistor count, and timing are presented.	Because implementation carried out at the transistor level and scaling for big input bit sizes is problematic. Unless the provided circuit is appropriately optimized during circuit design. The latency and dynamic power for big input bit sizes may be considerable .
Unary Processing based Low Power Sorter: [55] proposes a low-cost, low-power sorting algorithm based on unary processing. In large sorting networks, unary processing minimizes CAS connections.	45nm standard cell library is used to synthesize the proposed design. Power, area, and timing results are presented for different data widths.	Unary processing-based technique save a lot of power but add latency. It takes a long time to process digital unary streams.

Clock gating can be achieved by stopping the clock signals to the register files that is unutilized module by using an extra AND gate. This AND gate is controlled by an enable signal represented as Ena in Figure 3.5. There are two ways of representing extra AND gate with enabled control signal, one way is RTL and another way is using gate level netlist scripts. Automation [53] can be used to implement clock gating without disrupting the circuit operation. Figure 3.5 shows the clock gating representation with Data signal, enable signal, clocking signal and gated clock using AND logical gate.

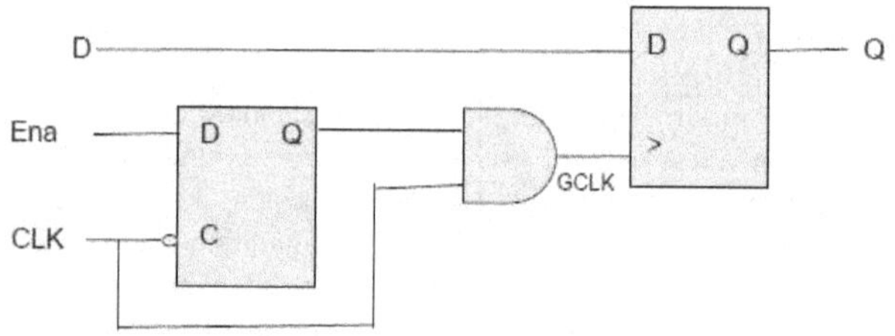

Figure 3.5: Schematic representation of clock gating

The register must only accept a new value on the rising edge of the clock and the gate is high for a clock to be correctly gated. If the clock is high, simply ANDing the clock and the enable together will result in a false clock on the rising edge of the gate.

3.2.2 Implementation

There are two ways of sorting: sequential circuit and combinational circuit. Generally, sorting networks follow combinational circuits and results in slow operation compared to sequential circuit. In the proposed technique, basic pipelining of sorting networks is used to speed up the operation [56]. There is huge sequence of comparators used between inputs and outputs in sorting circuit. To overcome the problems of huge number of comparators, pipelining techniques is used. Pipelining ensures the clocked register/pipeline stage register between different stages.

The pipeline stages vary with the size of input and architecture. For example, 8 bit-element sorting network requires a pipeline of 6-stage, 16 bit-element sorting network requires a 10-

stage pipelining and 32-bit sorting network requires a pipeline of 15-stage and so on pipeline stages vary with the bit-width of elements. In the proposed work, pipelined versions of Bitonic sorting, odd-even sorting and bubble sorting are implemented in Verilog and simulations carried out in Cadence NCSim tool. Cadence Genus Synthesis tools are used to synthesize the designs, which are then verified in Cadence NCSim using the saed90nm library. Generally, Clock gating is implemented using PERL scripting, and the gated netlist is tested in Cadence NCSim for functionality.

3.2.3 Result Analysis

The results demonstrate the tradeoff between the traditional and suggested clock gated sorter designs considering parameters such as area, power, and performance. The number of slices and multiplier, the area of the FPGA-based hardware is estimated (MULT). The experiments are carried out in order to evaluate the performance of various sorter architectures by incorporating clock gating techniques. The detailed results of the parameters like area, timing and power for 8-bit, 16-bit and 32-bit width data are presented in Table 3.3. From Table 3.3, it is clear that due to clock gating there is a consistent area gain. All the experiments are carried out at 50MHz frequency. The main advantage of clock gating technique used in this work is; it does not impose a significant penalty/stall on area or timing.
The most delayed route between an input and an output is referred to as the critical path. Clock gating slightly adds glitches at the leading edge of the clock that is observed in Table 3.3. The circuit uses a lot of dynamic power, which is significantly reduced by the clock gating. Power reduction can be achieved due to following reasons: -

- During the idle phase, no power is dissipated.
- The gated clock circuitry saves power.
- The original design's logic on the enable circuits is eliminated.

From the Table 3.3 with the 50MHz frequency, it is proved that proposed sorting architectures with clock gating technique shows the power reduction of 47.5%. The extra overhead is 1.62% due to the clock gating which is highly negligible in modern deep sub-micron era. The clock gating is a highly structured low power technique which reduces dynamic power significantly without taxing area and performance (speed). And it is evident from the results presented in the table 3.3.

Table 3.3 Comparison of Area, Power and Timing of Proposed and Conventional Sorters

Sorter	Data Width (#bits)	Area in square microns (Synthesized @ 50 MHz)		Critical-Path @50MHz frequency (in nano seconds)		Dynamic Power Consumption(mW) (@50 MHz)		
		Conventional-Pipelined Sorter	Proposed Clockgated Sorter	Conventional Pipelined Sorter	Proposed Clock gated Sorter	Conventional Pipelined Sorter	Proposed Clock gated Sorter	Reduction (%)
Bitonic Sort	8	36456.23	35345.87	6.54	6.77	1.3	0.585	46.59
	16	74234.45	75456.78	6.90	6.72	1.47	0.71	48.90
	32	145667.3	144589.8	7.42	7.73	1.88	0.91	51.83
Odd-Even Sort	8	32762.34	30231.89	5.84	5.81	1.39	0.64	52.55
	16	63298.75	61234.98	5.98	5.63	1.62	0.71	46.90
	32	125987.6	122889.9	8.41	8.85	2.1	0.91	47.02
Bubble Sort	8	40014.59	38234.88	6.59	6.73	1.37	0.65	49.53
	16	81298.56	79126.38	7.37	7.56	1.68	0.84	52.48
	32	178238.3	174398.5	8.23	8.43	2.08	1.10	52.65

After clock gating for the three sorting architectures, an analysis is made running at range of clock frequencies and results are tabulated in Table 3.4. The experiments conducted using Saed90nm standard cell library. The average reduction of dynamic power is 50.21% between 20 MHz and 80 MHz frequency. A relative results of dynamic power reduction for Bitonic sorter is tabulated in Table 3.5.

Sorting technique used in [51] and [55] are based on Bitonic network. For 32-bit sorters, the approach presented in [55] reduces dynamic power by up to 89%. The dynamic power of the proposed low power technique for 32-bit sorter is reduced by 48.50%, which is comparatively better than the low power sorter technique reported in [51]. This [55] method provides a technique based on unary processing that necessitates the use of pre- and post-processing modules. The pre-processing modules/ post-processing modules are not included in the calculating dynamic power consumption.

Table 3.4 Comparison of Proposed and Conventional Sorters

Sorting logic (32-bit)	Frequency Operating in terms of MHz	Dynamic Power Consumption (mW)		
		Conventional-Pipelined Sorter	Proposed Clock gated Sorter	Reduction (%)
Bitonic Sort	20	1.76	0.82	46.59
	40	1.82	0.89	48.90
	60	1.91	0.99	51.83
	80	1.96	1.03	52.55
Odd-Even Sort	20	1.94	0.91	46.90
	40	2.02	0.95	47.02
	60	2.14	1.06	49.53
	80	2.21	1.16	52.48
Bubble Sort	20	1.88	0.99	52.65
	40	2.06	1.05	50.97
	60	2.18	1.12	51.37
	80	2.23	1.24	53.91

Table 3.5 Comparison of Dynamic Power consumption of proposed and existing schemes for Bitonic Sorter(32-bit)

Percentage of dynamic power reduction in comparison with conventional Bitonic Sorter (Unary processing) [55]	Percentage of reduction in comparison with conventional Bitonic Sorter (Low Power) [51]	Percentage of reduction in comparison with conventional Bitonic Sorter with Proposed Clock gated Bitonic Sorter
89%	37.01%	48.51%

3.2.4 Summary

There are two ways of implementing sorting: Software implementation and Hardware implementation.

1. Software implementation such as on CPUs and GPUs consumes more number of machine cycles to sort given elements and
2. Hardware implementation such as on FPGA or ASIC gives much improvement in sorting.

There are various sorting techniques, among them Bitonic sorting, Bubble sorting and Odd-Even sorting are best suitable on hardware design. While designing sorters on hardware, the primary concerns is to improve performance and reduce power consumption. In this proposed work, on three separate hardware sorting networks, a well-known clock-gating technique is employed to produce low power consumption, and the trade-off factors like area, timing, and power consumption is examined.

Comparative results are reported for clock gated sorting designs versus previous low power sorting techniques. The recommended clock gated sorters use 47.51% less dynamic power than standard (non-clock gated) sorting circuits. A variety of frequencies are explored for the clock gating technique on sorters, and it is found that as the frequency of operation increases and the dynamic power consumption of the suggested clock gated sorters gradually decreases. The described clock gated strategy significantly lowers the dynamic power consumption of three widely used sorting processes when compared to traditional methods.

3.3 Modified Sorter Design with Structured Low Power techniques

The dynamic power is increased through pipelining and parallel processing, which has emerged as one of the main issues in contemporary data centres. Three significant sorting algorithms: odd-even sorting, bubble sorting, and Bitonic sorting are the main topics of this work. By using pipelined sequential implementations of odd-even sorting and Bitonic sorting, as well as structured low power techniques like clock gating, it is possible to examine the dynamic power for ASIC design. To the best of our knowledge, sorting networks use a general, well-established clock gating and multi-Vth (threshold) technique to cut power usage and optimize the key pathways. The comparative results for several sorters for power, performance, and area are reported in this chapter.

3.3.1 Modified Compare and Swap Unit

Figure 3.6 depicts the modified Compare and Swap (CAS) circuit diagram. An XOR gate is added to the basic CAS circuit shown in Figure 3.1 to enhance its performance. Direction signal is fed into a two-input XOR gate as an external input, and the comparator's output is fed into the XOR gate's other input. To execute ascending or descending order sorting, the direction signal is added to the sorter [93].

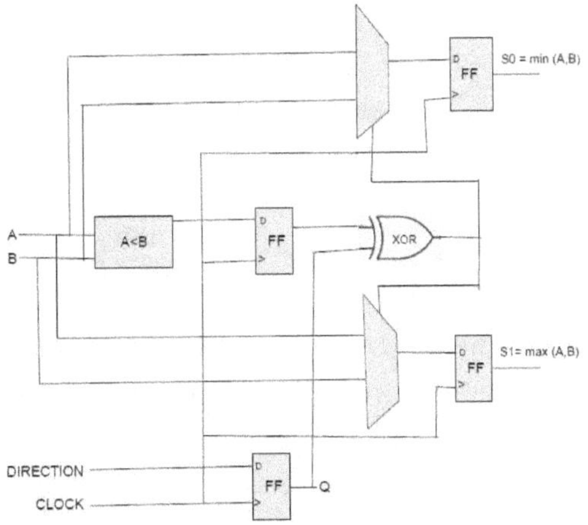

Figure 3.6: Modified CAS

The combinational CAS circuits that are frequently used in sorters will generally have the following problems:

- During gate level simulation and post layout simulation, the output of CAS circuits is not synchronized and does not match the output of the multiplexer. The outputs of the multiplexers must be clocked in order to guarantee the mismatches between them.
- The direction signal input into the XOR gate in the combinational CAS circuit is completely asynchronous, and it must be synchronous to prevent mismatches and ensure proper functionality of the circuit as a whole.

Both asynchronous inputs and outputs are clock-synchronized in the proposed improved CAS circuit, which is fully synchronous. This dramatically enhances functionality of CAS unit. The synthesis and simulation mismatches are decreased by transforming the massive combinational, unclocked CAS into a sequential CAS. A sequential CAS is used in place of the combinational CAS, as seen in figure 3.6. In this work, Bubble, Bitonic, and Odd-Even sorters are implemented using modified sequential CAS.

3.3.2 Structured low power techniques

Low power requirements can be met at the various level, listed as follows:

i. Circuit level
ii. Gate level
iii. RTL level
iv. System level.

This is a broad topic. Adopting the circuit level adjustments in a semi-custom design is challenging. Improvements at the level of logic gates are similarly challenging because semi-custom designs rely on foundry standard cell libraries that are already accessible. After several years of research, the industry has chosen low power solutions that are well-developed, easily adaptable to semi-custom design flows, and don't require any changes to the design or architecture. Clock gating, Power gating, and the use of Multi VDD and Multi Vth (Threshold Voltage) libraries are some examples of these techniques. Clock gating and multi-threshold are the only structured low power strategies used in this study on sorters. The structured low power techniques are described as follows:

1. Clock gating: simply turning off the clock signal while the circuit is not in use, lowers dynamic power dissipation.
2. Power gating: technique used for designing integrated circuits that save power consumption by cutting off the current to inactive circuit blocks.
3. Multi-VDD: It is used to conserve the design's dynamic and static power and actually uses many voltage domains in the same system without compromising speed.

4. Multi-Vth: This method uses Low Vth/High Vth cells while minimizing leakage power. Basic operation of this technique are reduce threshold gates on the critical path and larger threshold gates off the critical path.

3.3.2.1 Clock gating

Most designs only occasionally load data into the registers while continuously feeding the clock signal. Every pre-specified cycle will result in a continuous switching of the clock signal. The massive capacitive load is driven by the clock signal, which makes the clock a significant cause of power dissipation due to switching activity. Clock gating can be applied to a set of memory unit known as flip-flops. In this design clock are enabled by the control unit sending suitable signal that eliminates the necessity for extra clock toggles. When the register is turned off using the gating function, the circuit make sure that no power is lost during the time it is inactive. The gated clock network reduces dynamic power usage. An additional AND gate is managed by an enable signal and also used to disable the clock to the register files in idle module. Using scripts, additional AND gates and enable control signals can be added to RTL level or the gate level netlist. Figure 3.6 depicts the conceptual clock gating diagram.

3.3.2.2 Multi-threshold libraries

Each standard cell in standard cell libraries has a separate MOS device threshold voltage. Different power and speed parameters are supported by the majority of common cell libraries. The Vth (Threshold voltage) of the logic gate, together with other factors like transistor size, determines the power and speed of the cell. The classes of cells known as High Vth (HVth), Standard Vth (SVth), and Low Vth (LVth) are often supported in libraries. The table 3.6 lists the characteristics of the three various multi-Vth cells. The HVth cells have less speed, less dynamic power, and reduced leakage. The most leakage, dynamic power, and smallest delays will be found in LVth cells. SVth cells will operate at normal speeds and with typical power requirements.

Table 3.6 Features of Multi-Vth cells

Vth	Leakage Power	Dynamic Power	Speed
LVth	Highest	Highest	Highest
SVth	Normal	Normal	Normal
HVth	Lowest	Lowest	Lowest

3.3.3 Implementation

The multi-threshold voltage approach is classified as follows:

i. Standard Vth

ii. Low Vth

iii. High Vth

In this method, the critical path uses low threshold gates whereas the non-critical path uses high threshold gates. With this technology, operation speed is increased without an increase in power usage. Low and high Vth cells have the same area as standard Vth cells. Therefore, Standard Vth cells can be replaced with Low Vth or High Vth cells depending on the requirement in the critical paths or in any other paths of the design. With this method, performance is enhanced without compromising area or increasing power usage.

Multiple methods can be used to implement multi-Vth. It can be carried out by an engineering change order during layout, RTL synthesis, or at the gate level. The process of converting RTL Verilog code to functionally comparable gate-level netlist is known as logic synthesis. To achieve multiple Vth cells for various timing paths in the design, the standard cell libraries with multiple Vth can be employed in synthesis. The best location to implement multi-Vths is during synthesis. Utilizing the Standard Vth (SVth) library, synthesis is carried out.

In this study, clock gating and multi-Vth are used to create three sorters. The method used to implement clock gating is described above. The following is how multi-Vth implementation for sorters is carried out: -

- After RTL synthesis, clock gating is carried out. For functional verification, the clock gated gate level circuit created by synthesis is simulated. Standard Vth (SVt) library is used for synthesis with typical design constraints.

- Static Timing Analysis is performed to identify the critical section or collection of critical paths during the design process. We may examine the delay of each path in the design with the help of Static Timing Analysis.
- Designate high, medium, and low slack pathways among the design paths. Based on the slack value of each path, the categorization of paths is done. The road with the least slack, which is also a crucial path, is categorized in the low slack category. Similarly, all other paths are classified as high, medium, or low slack based on how much slack they have. Utilizing the SVth library, design is synthesized.
- In addition, higher Vth (High Vth) cells are used in place of the regular Vth cells for non-critical pathways (paths with high slack). The regular Vth cells are swapped out with LVth cells on important pathways, which have the least amount of slack.
- Neither HVth nor LVth cells are used to replace the standard cells that are shared by two or three timing paths. The standard Vth cells behave normally.
- The cells in the generated gate level netlist are customized using PERL scripts.
- Cadence Genus and Tempus tools are used to perform synthesis and static timing analysis respectively. Synopsys Saed90nm is used for synthesis.

3.3.4 Result analysis

3.3.4.1 Benchmarks

In the majority of enterprise applications, sorting takes up to 20% of the computing hardware resources. Additionally, a number of sorting algorithms are designed for general-purpose CPUs, GPUs, and FPGA deployment. A sorting method that functions well on multicore processors could not function well on FPGAs or dedicated ASICs. Sorting benchmark programmes were developed and described in [94] to evaluate and assess the performance of the sorting techniques. The existing benchmarks [94] were not designed to evaluate sorting algorithms based on FPGAs or specialized ASICs; instead, they focus mostly on general-purpose CPUs and GPGPUs.

Regardless of the hardware target, the programs/benchmarks used to evaluate the sorting algorithms must have some statistical characteristics like Gaussian distribution and collectible system statistics like I/O utilization, according to the authors in [94]. They argue for a comprehensive framework for sorting benchmarks and suggest that sorting benchmarks must be designed targeting the intended target like FPGA, GPGPU, or CPU.

The existing benchmarks in [94] are developed for CPUs and GPUs and are not helpful for evaluating FPGAs or ASICs. In this work, the micro benchmark was designed with the following statistical properties to evaluate the implementation of sorting strategies (Bubble, Bitonic, and Odd-even) for power consumption.

- Micro benchmark has 512 test vectors, with a choice of different bit width for each vector. In order to ensure 50% randomness, the input vectors are fed successively through sorters. Each vector will therefore have an equal number of ones and zeros. To achieve the maximal switching activity in the circuit and enable more precise measurement of maximum dynamic power, the uniformity in each vector is set to 50%.
- Each vector is fed into the sorters in order, checked for proper operation, and a switching activity file (VCD) is generated.

3.3.4.2 Experimental analysis with Clock gating

The investigations are conducted to evaluate the performance of several hardware sorters employing clock gating (multi-Vth not included). The switching activity and dynamic power for the suggested benchmark are generated using the micro benchmark outlined in the section above. Table 3.3 shows the findings for area, time, and power for a 50 MHz operating frequency. The synthesis is carried out at a frequency of 50 MHz, and gate level simulations are carried out to produce switching activity at various frequencies. Values for power consumption are recorded and shown in table 3.3.

3.3.4.3 Experimental analysis with Multi-Vth

By applying the multi-Vth and clock gating structured low power approaches to three different sorters, and the outcomes are given. Improved throughput without adding in dynamic power is the main goal of the multi-Vth deployment. Table 3.7 clearly shows that the critical path has been significantly reduced, allowing us to operate the design at higher frequencies across the PVT (Process, Voltage, Temperature) corners. The dynamic power usage for both clock gating and multi-Vth with clock gating at various frequencies is also shown in table 3.8. Table 3.7 clearly shows that the improvement in the critical path without compromising the power/energy consumption reduction brought about through clock gating is constant across frequencies.

Table 3.7 Comparison of Timing and Power of Proposed (with Clock gating/Multi-Vth) and Conventional Sorters

Sorter	Data Width (#bits)	Critical Path operating @ 50 MHz Frequency (in nano seconds)				Dynamic Power Consumption (mW) (@50 MHz frequency)				
		Conventional Pipelined Sorter	Proposed Clock gated Sorter	Proposed Clock gated with multi-Vth Sorter	Reduction using Clock gated with multi-Vth(%)	Conventional Pipelined Sorter	Proposed Clock gated Sorter	Proposed Clock gated with multi-Vth Sorter	Reduction using Clock gated (%)	Reduction using Clock gated with multi-Vth(%)
Bitonic Sort	8	6.54	6.77	4.23	64.69	1.3	0.58	0.58	46.59	45.31
	16	6.9	6.72	4.78	69.41	1.47	0.71	0.67	48.9	45.71
	32	7.42	7.73	5.98	80.57	1.88	0.91	1.01	51.83	53.77
Odd-Even Sort	8	5.84	5.81	3.91	66.93	1.39	0.64	0.65	52.55	46.97
	16	5.98	5.63	4.23	70.69	1.62	0.71	0.68	46.9	42.53
	32	8.41	8.85	5.82	69.20	2.1	0.91	1.10	47.02	52.42
Bubble Sort	8	6.59	6.73	4.43	67.17	1.37	0.65	0.66	49.53	48.32
	16	7.37	7.56	4.78	64.81	1.68	0.84	0.84	52.48	50.53
	32	8.23	8.43	5.92	71.94	2.08	1.12	1.21	52.65	58.17

Table 3.8 Dynamic Power Consumption of Proposed sorters (with Clock gating/Multi-Vth) and Conventional Sorters

Sorter 32-bit	Operating Frequency (MHz)	Dynamic Power Consumption (mW)				
		Conventional Pipelined Sorter	Proposed Clock gated Sorter	Proposed Clock gated with multi-Vth Sorter	Reduction (Clock gated) (%)	Reduction (Clock gated with Multi-Vth) (%)
Bitonic Sort	20	1.76	0.82	0.89	46.59	50.57
	40	1.82	0.89	0.94	48.9	51.64
	60	1.91	0.99	1.05	51.83	54.97
	80	1.96	1.03	1.11	52.55	56.68
Odd-Even Sort	20	1.94	0.91	0.98	46.9	50.51
	40	2.02	0.95	1.06	47.02	52.47
	60	2.14	1.06	1.19	49.53	55.61
	80	2.21	1.16	1.22	52.48	55.21
Bubble Sort	20	1.88	0.99	1.1	52.65	58.51
	40	2.06	1.05	1.18	50.97	57.28
	60	2.18	1.12	1.21	51.37	55.51
	80	2.23	1.24	1.29	53.91	57.84

3.3.4.4 Comparison

In Table 3.9, comparative findings for the relevant approach (Bitonic sorter) reduction in dynamic power are shown. Bitonic sorting is the foundation of both [51] and [55]. For a 32-bit sorter, the method suggested in [55] greatly reduces the dynamic power by up to 89%. The

low power sorter reported in [51] is outperformed by the suggested Clock gated sorter for 32-bit width, which lowers the dynamic power by 48.51%. The method described in [55] relies on unary processing, which necessitates pre- and post-processing modules. The pre- and post-processing modules are not considered in the computation of dynamic power.
When adopting multi-Vth cells, the critical paths in the three separate sorters are changed from SVth cells to LVth cells. The suggested low power bitonic sorter achieves a considerable decrease in power by 48.51% with clock gating and multi-Vth. Multi-Vth increases circuit speed by reducing the critical path. Clock gating with Multi-Vth cells has increased performance without compromising dynamic power consumption. The comparisons between the proposed sorters and the prior sorters are shown in Table 3.8.

Table 3.9 Comparison of Dynamic Power consumption of proposed and existing schemes for Bitonic sorter (32-bit)

Percentage of dynamic power reduction in comparison with conventional Bitonic Sorter (Unary processing) [55]	Percentage of reduction in comparison with conventional Bitonic Sorter (Low Power) [51]	Percentage of reduction in comparison with conventional Bitonic Sorter with Proposed Clock gated Bitonic Sorter	Percentage of reduction in comparison with conventional Bitonic Sorter with Proposed Clock gated with Multi-Vth Bitonic Sorter
89%	37.01%	48.51%	48.36%

3.3.5 Summary

The literature review makes it clear that Bitonic sorting, Bubble sorting, and Odd-even sorting are the best non-merge sorting strategies for hardware implementation. Designing sorting strategies for hardware implementation raises considerations about performance enhancements and power consumption reduction. In this dissertation, the trade-off factors like area, timing, and power consumption is investigated. To accomplish low power consumption on three different hardware suitable sorting algorithms, we used well-established structured low-power techniques including clock gating and multi-Vth.

To further minimize the critical path or enhance the frequency, multi-Vth libraries are used. The recent sorting architectures are compared and contrasted with the clock gating low-power technique, and comparative findings as shown. Multi-Vth implementation will minimize the critical path without threatening the clock gating-achieved reduction in dynamic power consumption. Comparing the proposed clock gated sorters to conventional (non-clock gated) sorting circuits, the dynamic power consumption is reduced by 47.5%. An investigation of the clock gating low-power technique on various sorters for different range of frequencies are made in this chapter. The results show that, dynamic power consumption of the proposed architecture lowers progressively as frequency increases. Hence, by applying low power technique on mentioned three sorters reduces dynamic power consumption compared to older methods.

Chapter 4

Comparison-Free Odd-Even Merge Sorter

These days, interesting applications like the Internet of Things (IoT), Robotics, and others are especially in need of hardware accelerators. Again sorting plays a vital role in accessing data from database. As discussed in chapter 3, there are efficient sorters that can be implemented on hardware like FPGA, ASIC and GPU. Researchers have also discovered a sorter method known as a comparison-free sorter that does not use a comparator or sophisticated circuitry without disturbing the performance.

This chapter consists of: Definition of Comparison-free sorters and its complexity, Literature survey of Comparison-free Sorters describing technique and implementation methodology, a novel hardware sorting engine and performance analysis and finally summarizing the methodology.

4.1 Introduction

Commercially available RISC-based microprocessors, such as ARM, Atmel-AVR, and many others, are now mostly used in embedded systems. This trend has been going on for several decades. IoT devices and energy-constrained embedded systems are just two applications that have made use of processors from the aforementioned families [9].

Many research teams around the world have created different kinds of RISC-V instruction sets, making them freely available for embedded devices. The RISC-V instruction set supports this, since it is an open platform for collaboration and successful attempts have been made to bring together businesses from various industries throughout the world.

With an open license, the business strategy is adaptable with the goal of allowing anyone to contribute to improvements or use contributions wherever [35]. This has aided research teams in implementing cutting-edge techniques to change the RISC-V architecture and produce a hardware accelerator. The General Purpose Registers (GPR), Control and Status Register

(CSR), ALU, Multiplier, and many more significant parts are among the many different building components that make up the RISC-V architecture.

Prefetch is one of the important CPU modules; it is configured to interpret commands read from memory and display the obtained instructions to the other processor blocks. Sorting is one of the fundamental building elements for carrying out the desired operation in the prefetch. However, sorting is important since it helps with query processing and many types of data sorting; examples of its application include data centres, data mining, IOT edge nodes, and cloud servers [36]. The majority of the data that arrives at data center will be in an alphabetical/numeric format. Sorting has the clear advantage of facilitating easy access to the database.

As a result, FPGAs have seen increased use in fields requiring complicated computations. Look-Up Tables, memory units, and small-scale functional units are the fundamental building blocks of FPGA and provide the benefit of programming simplicity [37]. Accelerators are essential because they enable parallel computing, which results in high processing, low latency, and low power consumption.

Several sorting algorithms have been created and passed through testing in recent decades for a variety of applications. The enhanced sorter's application domain is fairly broad, and it has a lot of potential to be used in many different ways. It has been observed that it is easier to verify the written algorithm in a software platform. Although configuring and executing it is difficult, it is also feasible to show on a hardware platform in which the results will be compared in terms of relative performance assessment. The data size, count of data elements, speed and the runtime are evaluated for comparability with the optimal algorithm.

4.2 Comparison-free sorters and its Overview

FPGA are designed to manage huge data sets, which is subjected to process like aggregating, sorting, merging, and joining to provide useful information. In the prior chapter, the significance of the sorting algorithm was covered. There are numerous sorting methods, including Bitonic sorter, Odd-Even sorter, Bubble sorter, Merge sorter, and Insertion sorter, each of which has pros and cons that are thoroughly explained in [72].

One of the simple and well-known methods [95] for sorting elements is the bubble sort, which offers a workable solution for a limited number of inputs. The iterative process starts by comparing two numbers, if the numbers are out of order, they will be switched as necessary, and this procedure will be performed repeatedly until the entire sequence has been completed. For an input of size M, sorting involves M comparisons in the first iteration, M-1 comparisons in the second, and so on until all of the elements have been sorted. O(M(M-1)/2) is a generalization of the complexity [96]. Less memory and fewer lines of code are required for this method during execution, but its main limitation is the more time it takes, and it is clear that the technique is quite inefficient for huge data sets.

A tree-based merge sorter was developed by Usui et al. [32] and successfully implemented for large-scale sorting. It was noted that the performance suffered due to the skewed data. A reliable method was required to manage large data sets. It was accomplished by putting into place an improved sort-merge unit, which increased throughput overall but was challenging to scale for a huge data sets.

The detailed comparison of several sorting methods is provided by Casper et al. [97]. The sorter that is free from a comparator method is the parameter that is focused. There have recently been numerous attempts to create comparator-free sorter, demonstrating attention to speed and resource usage. Similar to this, optimization is carried out in the suggested technique without requiring any comparator or complex data path [97].

Odd-Even sorting technique is an alternative sorter algorithm that, with a few minor changes, is extremely similar to bubble sorting. The process is executed until the array members are sorted, and there are two phases—the odd and even phases—occur throughout each iteration. This technique subsequently uses bubble sorting logic. Then bubble sort applied on odd indexed elements in the odd phase and even indexed ones in the even phase [98].

As long as no swapping operation is carried out, this process is repeated for the alternating index (odd/even pairs, even/odd pairs), leading to the array being in sorted form. The compare and swap modules are also a part of this sorting process. Therefore, $O(N^2)$ can be used to represent the timing complexity. This sorting method can be made to have an O(N) time complexity by adding parallel computing [99]. It has recently been discovered that this is the best sorting technique for hardware devices since it maintains performance over skewed data distributions while presenting stable throughput.

A common parallel technique for sorting, Bitonic sort is based on the Bitonic sequence. A Bitonic sequence pattern consists of almost half the array in ascending order and the remaining half in descending order [100]. Compared to odd-even sort, this sorting logic of bitonic sequence structure makes it easier to implement, hence it is extensively employed. This sorting method has a complexity of O (N $\log_2$(N)).

In the insertion sort, comparison of existing items carried out to identify the right node for placing a new element. The right node displays the smallest/largest item depending on whether the elements required in ascending/descending order. This information was sequentially scanned from right to left. In this sorting, the sorting process overlaps with the incoming data activities. This sorting method's primary problem is that it is inappropriate for massive amounts of data.

In comparison to other algorithms, the selection sorting algorithm is a straightforward algorithm for analysis. As a result, it is a sorting algorithm that is very simple to comprehend and is very helpful when working with a limited number of elements. However, due to its complexity being O (N^2), where N is the number of entries in table, it is ineffective for sorting a huge data set. Because it chooses the smallest number of elements in each step of the sorting process, this algorithm is known as Selection Sort. Fixing the minimal value at index 0 is a crucial function of the selection sort. The value is changed to the middle position after looking for the list's minimum entry. To obtain a sorted array, it is then necessary compute and increment the minimum index and repeat the process.

Another commonly used sorting technique is merge sorter. Merge sort can be used if there are huge data sets [101] and bubble sort works best for a small data set. Because merge sort is ineffective for storing items in RAM for huge data sets, it turns to a hybrid sort-merge strategy. Additionally, known as external sorting. Parallel merge sorting is supported by FPGA and reduces the time taken for sorting compared to convention sorting techniques.

Merges several 1000 sorted sequences in a single run [104] and uses a method that can merge up to 4096 sequences at a speed of 253 MHz with 64-bit keys. Techniques including speculative execution, pipelining of critical paths, streamlined inter-level tree interactions, and parameterizing stage sizes to allow trade-offs between utilization/throughput and stalling rates are implemented to achieve high throughput.

In comparator-free sorting, a comparator or sophisticated circuit are not necessary. Many of the comparison-free sorting architectures are just built using simple gates. Delay can therefore be overlooked, which enhances performance as a whole. A single bit comparator is a comparator that compares only one bit. Two inputs are provided for each pair of 1-bit numbers, and 3-outputs are provided to obtain less than, equal to, and greater than between two numbers.

The pictorial representation of 1-bit magnitude comparator is depicted in Figure 4.1.

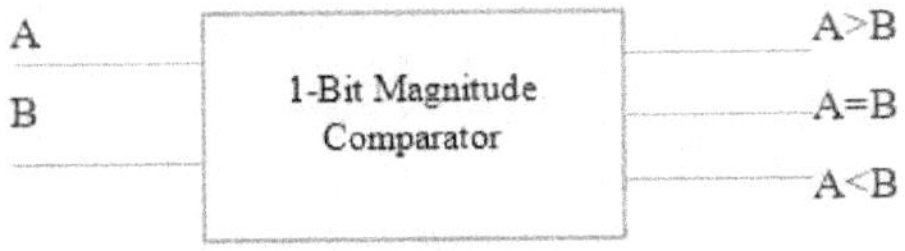

Figure 4.1 1-Bit Magnitude Comparator

The following Table 4.1 is a truth table for a 1-bit comparator:

Table 4.1 1-bit comparator truth table

A	B	A<B	A=B	A>B
0	0	0	1	0
0	1	1	0	0
1	0	0	0	1
1	1	0	1	0

For each output in the truth table above, the following Boolean expressions can be used:

A>B: AB'

A=B: A'B'+AB

A<B: A'B

Similarly, 2-bit, 4-bit, N-bit comparator can be designed by constructing truth table and deriving Boolean expressions. As the size of comparator increases, deriving Boolean expression and writing truth table becomes cumbersome. So alternate methods like K-map, Quine-McCluskey (QM) can be used to solve expression.

The other method of comparing elements can be achieved by 16-bit magnitude comparator using efficient full adders as shown in Figure 4.2.

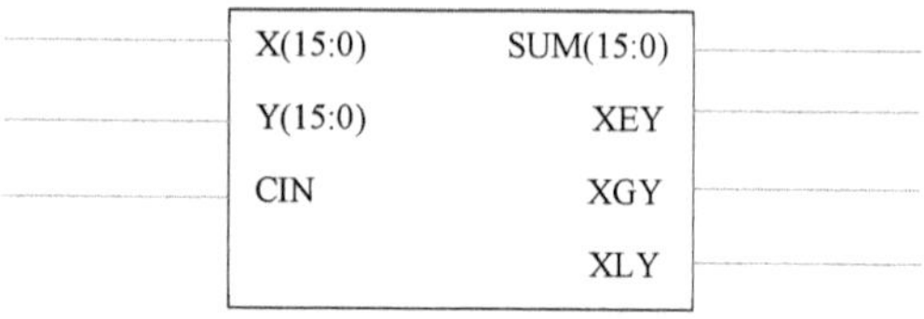

Figure 4.2 16-bit magnitude comparator

A 16-bit magnitude comparator is made using a 16-input AND gate, 16 1-bit efficient Full Adders, and a 2-input NOR gate. Inputs are present (X16, Y16 X15, Y15 and so on up to X1,Y1). where S and C are each Full Adder outputs. The total output from each Full Adder (S1 to S16) has been sent to the gate, whose output determines whether XEY. If XGY, output carry C16 will tell us. The NOR gate was given the two outputs, and its output determines whether the X inputs go to the 12-input OR gate and the XLY Y inputs go to the enable inputs of each comparator. Traditional 16-Bit comparator uses greater space, electricity, and delay. To overcome the problem of power, area and delay, the basic gates can be used.

Elements can be sorted using a variety of methods without a comparison unit by improving the performance of sorting methodology. Table 4.2 presents a detailed comparison-free sorting method, technology, and implementation approach. Based on the technique and standard cell library used, few of the remarks are drawn. Minimal power analysis is made and there is a lot of scope to improve power efficiency.

Table 4.2 Comparison of various comparison-free sorting techniques and methodologies

Technique	Technology, Implementation Methodology and Complexity	Remarks
Hardware–based sorting technique uses SRAM-based memory to store data elements [57]. The elements are stored in the form of Hamming maximum order representations.	90 nm TSMC technology. Matrix multiplication using AND operation sorts the data elements. The hardware structure reduces the data that flows in sorting network between the memory and sorting units. Complexity results in O(N) order.	Power Analysis - not reported The proposed sorting unit suitable for single core architecture.
Data elements are sorted on-the-fly without any comparators between the data [54]. Temporary registers are used to hold binary elements.	Matrix-mapping operation by transposing one-hot matrix to the size N×N elements and binary multiplication performed on input elements. This results in eliminating comparison operations to sort elements. Complexity of the order O (N).	The proposed algorithm reported power consumption of 1.60 mW for 1024 input elements. Not suitable for large set of elements.
Null convention logic (NCL) unit is proposed [58]. The comparison-free unit designed using AND-OR gates and one-hot matrix multiplies with binary matrix.	The NCL sorting unit and comparison free unit compared with respect to transistor, LUTs and power.	When compared to null convention sorting, one-hot matrix comparison free sorting dramatically reduces total power, area, and time.
[59] Proposed a comparison-free sorting approach based on software that divides calculations into three phases: count, Add and sort.	In each stage, grouping threads so that it can execute single-instruction at a time. This is a requirement for maximizing hardware resource usage. CPU implementations are based on a mathematical algorithm (single thread, multi-thread)	Power analysis not reported
In the first iteration of the suggested architecture, the largest element (LE) is discovered. The next LE is then determined from the remaining data set in each cycle. The sorting engine has selected blocks in a cascade fashion [60]. Each block in cascaded consists of N basic cells.	65-nm technology standard cell library. Delay is same as Linear sorting.	Tested successfully for 1024 elements of 32 bits and 2048 elements of 11 bits. Power consumption not discussed

Each cell made up of a 2-input AND gate and a tiny switch.		
Demultiplexer Array Sorting (DAS) engine- Using the radix-2 sort method in conjunction with the counting sort technique [61]. It performs bit-unit operations using a bit-serial technique, which is substantially lighter on the hardware than comparison-based versions that conduct word-unit operations.	DAS sorts N of k-bit data using an NXN deMUX array and completes the operation in k cycles, regardless of N. Time complexity of DAS is O(Nk). DAS has $O(N^2)$ hardware complexity due to the array of deMUX,	DAS requires very little memory because it doesn't relocate any data during sorting and instead regenerates input data in sorted order.
[62] Proposed FSM as a sorting algorithm which is free of comparison. It uses a single hot decoder and an up counter to sort elements and is based on counting the amount of ones.	90 nm CMOS technology Comparison-free sorting incorporated in FSM reduces the complexity on hardware devices.	Designed for signed numbers
Tree-based recursive algorithms using HFSM(Hierarchical Finite State Machine) [63]	HFSM has implicit modules. A single state stack plus a state register make up the system. Separate labels must be assigned to states in various modules in this case (different codes).	HFSM uses less hardware resources because of implicit modules. The modules become implicit, making updating and modifying them difficult.

Table 4.3 presents a survey on comparison-free sorting considering parameters like technology used for implementation, input size considered, variance operating frequency and finally advantages of technology and existing technique. From this table, in future it is easy for the researchers to decide the best technique and optimal operating frequency.

4.3 Novel Hardware Sorting Engine

The odd-even sorting method is intended for use with parallel computers. The pairs odd-even and even-odd are used to sort the data. The worst-case complexity represented by $O(N^2)$ and O(N) is the best-case complexity. FPGAs can effectively implement this sorting since they reduce the CPU's resource constraints. This sorting can alternatively be implemented on a

GPU for faster throughput, although FPGAs consume less power than GPUs. The odd-even sorting architecture uses a hierarchical approach, with sub-modules like move_through and swap_if_required being instantiated. The architecture of sorting algorithm is simple to understand because of the modular parameters.

Table 4.3 Comparison–free sorting survey including technology, input size and operating frequency and advantages

Technology	Input size and operating frequency	Advantages
The proposed designed [57] synthesized on 90 nm TSMC technology.	Input size of N=1024 elements and Operates at 0.25 GHz frequency.	Eliminates comparison unit and high power dissipation.
The proposed designed [54] synthesized on 90 nm TSMC technology.	Input size is 1024, size of each element is 10-bits operating at 0.5GHz frequency.	Execution time is comparatively less over other existing sorting techniques such as Quicksort, Bubblesort, mergesort and so on.
The comparison free sort unit synthesized using Xilinx ISE 12.1i and on Spartan-3 processor [58]	8-bit input size	A drastic improvement achieved by comparing with NCL technique.
CPU & GPU [59]	From 27 to 230 elements in input sizes, from all unique components to just one repeated element	Algorithm works efficiently in GPU compared to CPU
65-nm technology standard cell library. Simulated and synthesized in Xilinx ISE 14.7 [60]	Runs at an operating frequency of 125MHz.	doesn't need any kind of comparator, special circuitry, or a complicated computation. The sorting followed by storing of data is processed in a pipelined manner using just a few simple logic gates.
The simulation is performed by HSPICE. Model parameter : 1.2V-0.13μm 8RF-LM [61]	DAS sorts *N* data in *k* cycles regardless of *N*, but the clock cycle time is proportional to *N*.	DAS based sorting provides hardware-efficient implementation. its optimal memory requirement makes DAS a scalable architecture
Compiler designed using Synopsys DC and synthesis on Vivado [62]	Sorting for both negative and positive numbers	reduces power and area in comparison to the earlier design.
Simulated using Xilinx ISE 11 and deployed on FPGA Spartan3E-1200E-FG320 [63]	A random number generator generates 2^{11} datasets with a 14-bit length	FPGAs have good capabilities for accelerating and also suitable for recursive algorithms over data structures that resemble trees.

The basic gates in a simple circuit receive the even-odd indexed data items. Because of basic gates are used in the proposed architecture, the delay may be disregarded, which ultimately improves performance as a whole.

Algorithm 1 shows the step-by-step procedure for comparison-free technique applied to odd-even sorter. Unsorted elements are taken as input and output is sorted elements. Initially all the elements are passed to Move_through block. Next step, first element moved through without comparing or making any changes. Other elements are compared and swapped as per requirement of application. This process keeps repeating till the elements are in sorted order.

Algorithm 1 Odd_Even _Comparator_Free

Input given : in1, in2, in3, in4, in5

Output obtained: out1, out2, out3, out4, out5

1: All inputs passed to Move_Through

2: a. Move_Through(in1,out1)

b. Swap_If_Required(in2,in3,out2,out3)

c. Swap_If_Required(in4,in5,out4,out5)

3: a. Swap_If_Required(in1,in2,out1,out2)

b. Swap_If_Required(in3,in4,out3,out4)

c. Move_Through(in5,out5)

4: a. Move_Through(in1,out1)

b. Swap_If_Required(in2,in3,out2,out3)

c. Swap_If_Required(in4,in5,out4,out5)

5: a. Swap_If_Required(in1,in2,out1,out2)

b. Swap_If_Required(in3,in4,out3,out4)

c. Move_Through(in5,out5)

Algorithm 2 is to move the elements without modification.

Algorithm 2 Move_Through

Input: in

Output: out

out←in

Algorithm 3 explains how the swap operation carried out. Swap decision is based on the Boolean expression solved by Quine-McCluskey (QM) algorithm.

Algorithm 3 Swap_If_Required

Input: in_i, in_j

Output: out_i, out_j

1. y=Boolean_Expression(in_i, in_j)
2. if(y)
   a. $out_j \leftarrow in_i$
   b. $out_i \leftarrow in_j$

   else

   a. $out_j \leftarrow in_i$
   b. $out_j \leftarrow in_j$

Boolean Expression: By applying logical operations to the inputs, a Boolean expression generates a Boolean value. It is essential for creating algorithms, designing circuits, and programming applications. Therefore, reducing Boolean expression is a crucial requirement. The equation can be minimized using a variety of techniques, including the algebraic rules, the K-map, the tabular approach, and the Quine-McCluskey (QM) algorithm. The QM algorithm is the most effective and potent method for minimizing Boolean expression among these. The swap decision in the proposed design is determined based on the QM method's outcome. The function f produced the following prime implicants.

If(A>B)

then f=1;

else f=0;

where A, B are inputs to Swap_If_Required function.

Figure 4.3 depicts a brief overview diagram of the proposed architecture. The hardware engine takes an unsorted array as input and uses the odd-even comparator-free sorting technique to produce a sorted array. There are principally two benefits to this approach: Since basic gates are utilized in place of comparators, N elements are sorted in N-1 clock cycles with extremely minimal latency. The hardware engine is made up of enumerated blocks connected together in a cascaded fashion as shown in Figure 4.4. One block at a time are chosen. The proposed engine needs N blocks, including the first stage carry out operation, for N sets of n-bit wide arrays.

Figure 4.3 Proposed Architecture

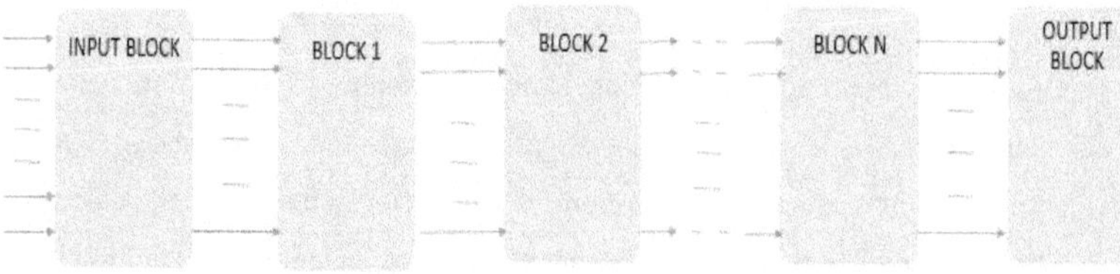

Figure. 4.4 Block diagram of Hardware Engine for Odd-Even Comparator Free Sorting

Figure 4.5 shows the internal architecture of each alternate block. Each block has two primary purposes: moving through and swapping out if necessary. The data is not changed as it is passed to the following block via the Move_through method. The Swap applies the Boolean expression to the input received, if necessary in a block. The switching takes place in accordance with the outcome of a Boolean expression, which uses comparator-free logic. Figure 4.6 depicts the detailed structure of the comparator free block as determined by a Boolean expression.

When the chip is turned on, the FPGA loads a unique truth table. LUT could be compared to a little RAM. LUTs are typically 6-input LUTs in size. Flip-flop and LUT-based reconfigurable chips are called FPGAs. LUTs are customized truth tables that are filled with pertinent values. LUTs can be used in several ways to mimic logic gates. The Look Up Table (LUT) and Multiplexer are utilized on FPGAs to quickly solve the Boolean statement. Hardware LUTs are truth tables that have been specially created and can be modified to do any necessary logic operations. As needed, the values are loaded into the FPGA. For any combinational circuit, LUTs can be tailored. LUT6 is utilized in the suggested structure. It is a LUT with 6 inputs and 1 output. Four LUT6 and three MUX, as seen in Figure 4.4, are used to resolve Boolean statements for comparator-free sorting.

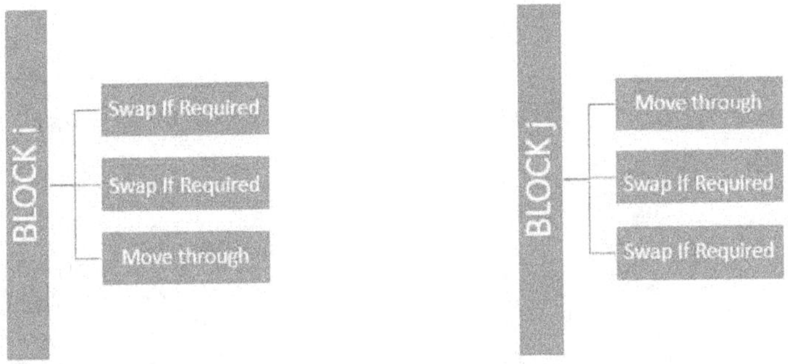

Figure 4.5 Internal structure of Alternate Blocks. Blocki and Blockj

Consider the following five data items as an example for sorting: 4(=0100), 7(=0111), 3(=0011), 5(=0101), and 2(=0010). The first element in the first stage is carried directly into the second stage without any modifications. Depending on what a Boolean expression returns, the even and odd indexed components are swapped. Elements 7 and 3 are present here. Since the Boolean statement returns 1, swapping takes place. The following two elements, 5 and 2, must be swapped. This procedure is repeated for the following pipeline stage. The final stage includes a sorted array. Figure 4.7 illustrates the proposed sorting algorithm with an example.

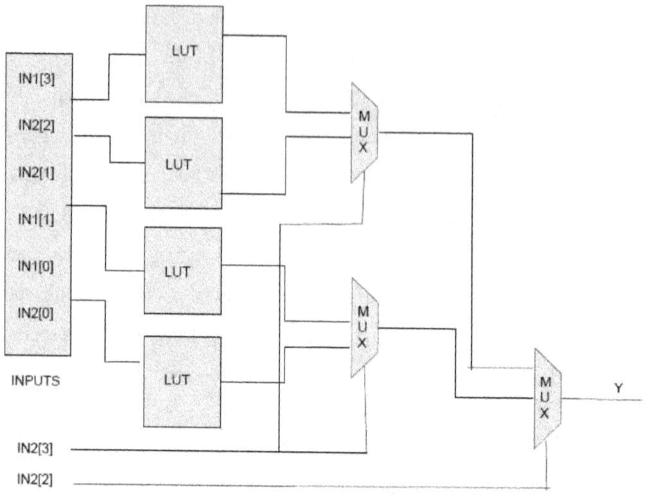

Figure 4.6 Structure of Comparator-Free Block

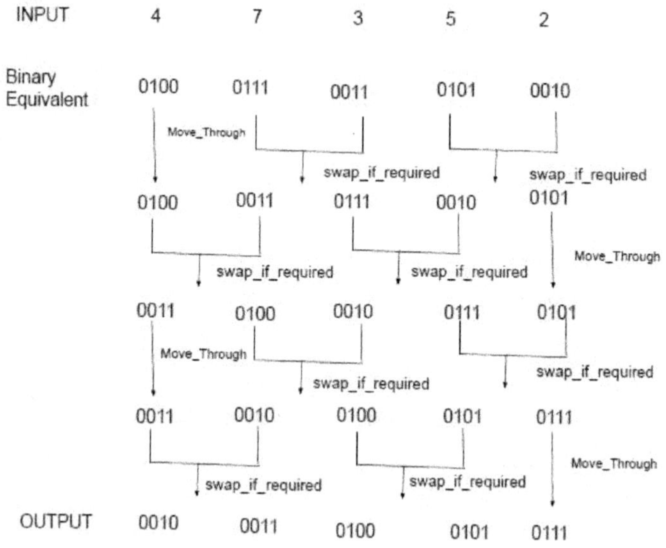

Figure 4.7 An example of N=5 elements illustrating the proposed sorting technique

4.4 Result Analysis

It has been demonstrated that the inclusion of hardware sorting units enhances the system's performance on sorting applications. To implement the addition of sorting units, more hardware resources are needed. These hardware resource costs are calculated as a percentage of the slices of look-up tables (LUTs) that were used, as reported by Vivado after implementation.

The designed sorter algorithmic program was simulated using Xilinx ISE 14.7 on Virtex-7; it is tuned and integrated for 28-nm for the best performance; and the complete specification of the board on which it was synthesized is xc7vx415tffg1158-1. The proposed sorter outcomes are contrasted with those of other sorter techniques, including range of parameters:

i. Bitonic sorter logic
ii. Insertion sorter logic
iii. Selection sorter logic
iv. Bubble sorter logic

The factors for comparison include:

i. Number of slices used
ii. Number of LUTs required
iii. Number of logic cells
iv. Number of LUT flip-flops memory
v. IO utilization
vi. Finally, delay

Table 4.4 lists the findings from the selected comparators as well as the proposed comparator. All tests were conducted at 224 MHz. Figure 4.8, 4.9, 4.10 and 4.11 shows the graphical representation of results by comparing resource parameters.

The number of elements considered for illustrating sorting technique is eight. Hence, N=8 in all conditions. Therefore, for 4-bit number the total length is 32-bits, for 8-bit numbers the total length is 64-bits, for 16-bit numbers total length is 128-bits, for 32-bit numbers the total length is 256-bits.

Table 4.4 Comparison of parameters of existing sorters with the proposed sorter for variable bit width

Width	Sorter Logic	Number of Slice Registers: (Out of 515200)	Number of Slice LUTs: (Out of 257600)	Number used as Logic (Out of 257600)	Number of LUT Flip Flop pairs used (%)	IO Utilization (350)	Delay: (ns)
4 bits	Bitonic	72	219	221	31	68	2.87
	Proposed Odd Even	**70**	**168**	**168**	**30**	**68**	**2.14**
	Insertion	70	168	168	41	68	2.49
	Selection	79	214	216	33	68	3.33
	Bubble	76	235	236	31	68	3.44
8 bits	Bitonic	140	430	436	33	134	3.43
	Proposed Odd Even	**134**	**284**	**284**	**28**	**132**	**3.10**
	Insertion	138	637	640	32	132	3.40
	Selection	145	378	382	38	132	3.74
	Bubble	145	395	400	37	132	3.47
16 Bit	Bitonic	264	650	652	41	260	4.69
	Proposed Odd Even	**262**	**491**	**491**	**37**	**260**	**3.79**
	Insertion	274	1087	1097	45	260	5.60
	Selection	270	645	646	42	260	4.86
	Bubble	273	678	679	41	260	5.94
32 bits	Bitonic	518	1536	1536	44	516	5.78
	Proposed Odd Even	**521**	**1052**	**1052**	**42**	**518**	**4.44**
	Insertion	620	2777	2867	46	516	5.87
	Selection	530	1150	1155	46	56	4.89
	Bubble	533	1331	1338	48	516	6.12

Sorting different bit-width (4-, 8-, 16-, 32-bits) with 8 elements, each case results in delays of 2.147 ns, 3.104 ns, 3.791 ns, and 4.445 ns for the proposed architecture, respectively. Additionally, it is clear that the proposed method/sorter uses fewer LUTs than the previous sorting methods. Therefore, it can be said that along with the decrease in time, the required space would also decrease. Hence, concluding that the proposed strategy outperforms the compared methods as a result.

The table 4.5 reports how the comparison-free odd-even unit method reduces LUT count and time delay. By considering the size of input as 8-bits and number of elements=3. The table 4.5 represents the comparison between null convention logic unit, existing comparison free sorting unit and Proposed Comparison-free sorter unit. In which comparison-free sorting produce the efficient output results. The highlight from table is delay, which is minimal and ignorable.

Table 4.5 Comparison results of NCL, Comparison-free sorter and Proposed Comparison-free sorter unit

Sl. No	Parameter	NCL [58]	Comparison-free sorter unit [58]	Proposed Comparison-free sorter unit
1	# of Slices	64	49	46
2	# of LUT	112	85	79
3	Delay (ns)	7.646	6.991	1.164

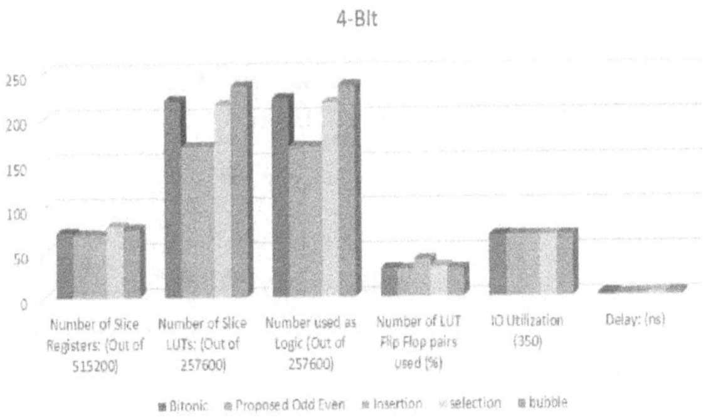

Figure 4.8 Comparison of the parameters like Number of Slices, Register, Number of LUTs, Flip-flops used, Delay for 4-bit sorters of different approaches

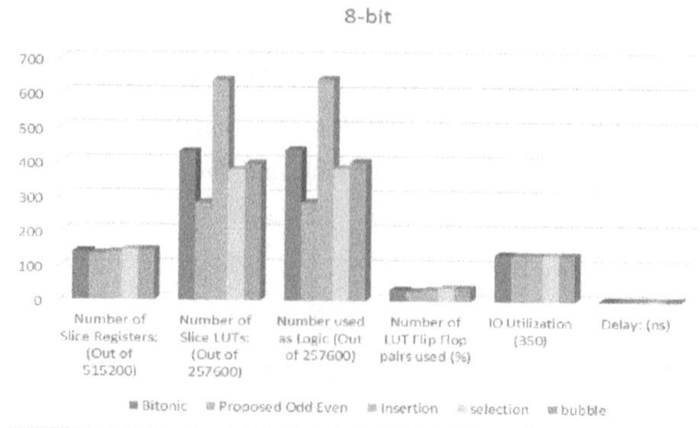

Figure 4.9 Comparison of the parameters like Number of Slices, Register, Number of LUTs, Flip-flops used, Delay for 8-bit sorters of different approaches

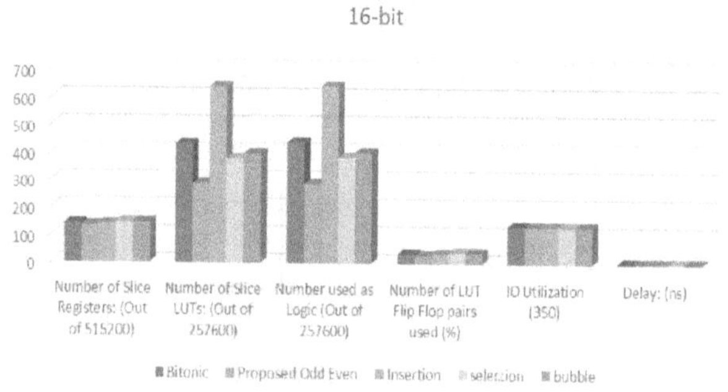

Figure 4.10 Comparison of the parameters like Number of Slices, Registers, Number of LUTs, Flip-flops used, Delay for 16-bit different sorters

Table 4.6 compares the proposed approach's utilization of FPGA resources to a number of previous sorting techniques, including [31], [54], [103], and [60]. In this table, proposed architecture consumes less resource for number of elements N=128 and each input size of 32-bits in width. The resource parameter considered for comparison among various sorting methods are Slices utilized, LUTs used and Flip-Flops required in pairs. The device used for simulation varies slightly, however the proposed architecture has high performance in terms of resource utilization. And one more important parameter considered in Table 4.6 is Delay in nanoseconds for all the sorting methods referred. Comparatively proposed architecture takes less time to sort elements.

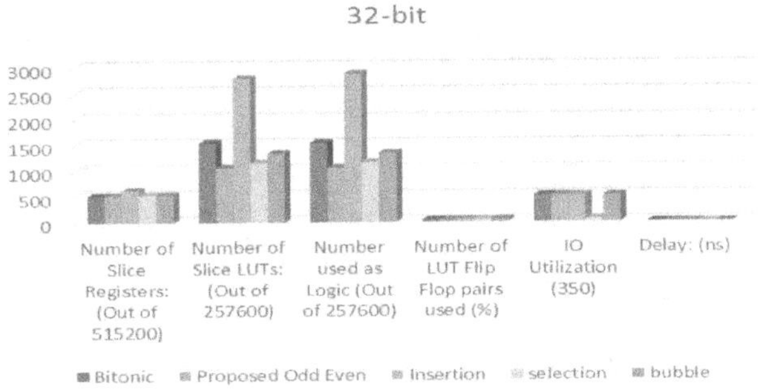

Figure 4.11 Comparison of the parameters like Number of Slices, Registers, Number of LUTs, Flip-flops used, Delay for 32-bit different sorters

Table 4.6 Usage of resources by various sorting methods for 128 elements/32-bits width

Parameter	[31]	[54]	[103]	[60]	Proposed
Slices Occupied	11142	1665	6832	504	336
LUTs Utilized	71310	3750	43719	2016	1682
Flip-Flops	90169	3330	133584	2016	672
Delay (ns)	400	1500	1600	1300	72
Device Name	Virtex-7	Virtex-5	Virtex-7	Virtex-5	Virtex-7

Table 4.7 shows how the proposed sorting engine uses resources when applied to a variety of data sets with different data widths. This table provides detailed resource utilization of proposed sorter logic. Width of elements considered are 8-bits, 16-bits and 32-bits. Number of elements varied as 256, 512 and 1024 as input sequence. Correspondingly the resource utilized and percentage of resource utilization with respect to slice registers, LUTs and Flip Flops are listed in table.

Table 4.7 Resource utilization of comparison-free odd-even sorter architecture

Parameter	Width	Elements(N)	Resource Used	% of Utilization
Slice Registers			4288	0.832
LUTs			9088	3.53
Flip Flops		256	4224	13.51
Slice Registers			8555	1.66
LUTs			18173	7.05
Flip Flops		512	8442	27.5
Slice Registers			17145	3.33
LUTs			36347	14.11
Flip Flops	8-bits	1024	16891	54.03
Slice Registers			8384	1.63
LUTs			15712	6.1
Flip Flops		256	8320	26.62
Slice Registers			16762	3.25
LUTs			31420	12.2
Flip Flops		512	13532	43.29
Slice Registers			33531	6.51
LUTs			62844	24.4
Flip Flops	16-bits	1024	21273	68.05
Slice Registers			16672	3.24
LUTs			33664	13.07
Flip Flops		256	6576	21.04
Slice Registers			33334	6.47
LUTs			67321	26.13
Flip Flops		512	20510	65.61
Slice Registers			66682	12.94
LUTs			134655	52.27
Flip Flops	32-bits	1024	24295	77.72

4.5 Summary

A modified comparison-free Odd-Even technique to sorting N elements is proposed in this chapter. The proposed sorting's complexity, which is used to indicate sorting speed, is O(N). The expanded even-odd sorter is tested and validated by implementing it on Virtex-7 configured FPGAs, which can operate at 224 MHz. It is clear from the comparison table that the suggested solution outperforms other options considering parameters like delay, area, power and IO utilization. This sorting procedure run in a superimposed manner as a result of channeling, which eliminates the requirement for an increase in memory cycles for the classification of the items.

The simulation results clearly show that even the smallest resource allocation was sufficient to surpass several modern hardware-based categorization techniques with only minimal sorting delay.

The important feature of FPGA is Reconfiguration. The reconfiguration time depends on the architecture and FPGA device chosen for the deployment. In my work, Xilinx ISE 14.7 on Virtex-7 is used and takes 8.7ns for reconfiguration. Reconfiguration depends on application and in my work, Static reconfiguration of FPGA is suitable.

In the future, the proposed pipelined structure will be used to take advantage of spatial parallelism and boost performance for large data sets. In conclusion, the suggested hardware classification approach may be a helpful embedded component that serves as an implementation accelerator for data awareness.

Chapter 5

An Effective Architecture to Implement Customized Sort Instruction in RISC-V Processor

Reduced Instruction Set Computer-Version V(RISC-V) provides entirely open-free accessible to both business and academia Instruction Set Architecture (ISA). In this chapter, main focus is on designing comparison-free sorter in RISC-V architecture. Among all the sorters, Odd-even sorter is efficient and can be implemented on hardware. A comparison-free unit is added to odd-even sorter to increase the performance.

This chapter consists of: Conventions of RISC-V microprocessor architecture, Literature survey of Sorters on RISC-V, and proposed novel sorter on MicroBlaze soft core processor, the result analysis of sorter considering parameters like power consumption and resource utilization.

5.1 Conventions of RISC-V microprocessor architecture

After several years and a large number of projects using MIPS, SPARC, and x86 as the research basis, it is time to look at ISA for the following set of initiatives. Therefore, the logical choices were x86 and Advanced RISC Machine (ARM). Due to its complexity and Intellectual Property (IP) problems, X86 processor was not possible solution. Advanced RISC Machine (ARM) processor is not feasible as there are no 64-bit, complicated, or Intellectual Property (IP) issues. RISC-V are successfully built using RISC concepts on an open standard Instruction Set Architecture (ISA). A new architecture called RISC-V is accessible under open, free, and unrestrictive licenses.

Since RISC-V is a set of specifications rather than a processor in and of itself. it is essential to choose which version of the architecture is utilized for implementation. The RISC-V architecture is implemented in a variety of hardware platforms with varying functions, sizes, and operating frequencies, but the fundamental instruction set remains constant. As long as the programmes don't require any extra instructions, different RISC-V implementations can run the identical applications. Micro architectural level advancements are widely experimented with RISC-V due to its modularity.

5.1.1 About RISC-V/ RISC-V Basics

A genuine ISA, not just a simulation or binary translation, that can be implemented directly on native hardware. An ISA that supports effective implementation in any of these but preventing the over-architecture for a specific microarchitecture style (such as microcoded, in-order, decoupled, or out-of-order) or deployment technology (such as full-custom, ASIC/FPGA). An ISA divided into optional standard extensions and a small base integer ISA for general-purpose software development. This small base integer ISA can be used alone as a base for educational or customized accelerators. [64] this architecture supports various ISA versions implemented on different bit width. Only 47 instructions of RISC-V resulted in foundation of RISC-V (RV32I). The specifications provided in RISC-V improves the ISA by altering these instructions as per the user requirement [65].

Modularity was a major consideration when developing RISC-V [65]. As a result, not every RISC-V processor is required to support the entire specification. One may be content with simply some fundamental capabilities if they are creating a low power embedded device. Additionally, general-purpose computers require different things than research- and supercomputers. As a result, RISC-V was designed to have a minimal base and the ability to be expanded with additional modules. On the other hand, a hardware accelerator has benefits such being simpler to design and maintaining processor core compliance along the fundamental ISA in RISC-V. The benefit provided in hardware accelerator, constant processing is possible with any processor provided there is a dedicated interconnection between the main processor and the co-processor (considered as hardware accelerator).

When using an FPGA, some physical limitations must be taken into consideration. Most importantly, the functionality stated in code must be implemented within the constrained area provided by FPGAs, which is typically determined by the count of logic cells they contain. Designer ensure that the FPGA can accommodate both a RISC-V CPU and an extra hardware accelerator. Due to their soft processors and capacity for quick reconfiguration, Field-Programmable Gate Array (FPGA) devices can take benefit of its flexible hardware. This allows for the selection of a relatively small RISC-V core, leaving the accelerator portion with the maximum number of logic cells.

5.1.2 Soft-core processor and its features

A soft-core processor is a model of a particular processor (CPU) in hardware description language (HDL) that may be altered for a specific application and synthesized for an ASIC or FPGA target. Designers can use HDLs to develop customizable Intellectual Property (IP), sometimes known as Intellectual Property cores. This utilizes the reusable parts to build and define hardware functionality. In order to provide desired functionality, IP cores are instantiated within the design. Both within a single design and throughout various design projects, this cores can be applied multiple times. Popular IP cores that are coupled to FPGA processors embed with UARTs, Ethernet, and processing units. Soft-core processors offer various benefits over specially developed processors in many applications. Benefits such as lower cost, flexibility, platform independence, and increased resistance to degradation are provided by soft-core processors. A specific task is carried out by embedded systems, which are made up of both hardware and software components. Typically, they have embedded processors, which frequently take the form of soft-core processors and run software.

Making a decision on a soft processor core can be difficult and have an important influence on the design. The following are some of the most important factors to consider when choosing an FPGA soft processor core:

- Implementation costs
- Operational effectiveness
- Usage of power
- Tools for design and development
- Considerations for operating systems

- Options and capacity for debugging
- Materials from the manufacturer and technical assistance

These design elements are covered in more detail in the sections that follow.

Costs: The cost of a proposed solution is frequently the first factor taken into account considering the great most of projects based on embedded design. The price of the final product depends on the costs associated with developing the hardware and software as well as the materials and manufacturing processes. First, a cost analysis that considers the possible advantages of FPGA technology must be done in order to assert using a soft processor core during design. An embedded FPGA soft processor solution is further considered after this evaluation.

Operational effectiveness and power: The operating performance and power needed to accomplish the intended system functionality are two potentially crucial system characteristics. There will usually be a difference in power consumption and performance levels between processor implementations and FPGA-based soft processor cores.

Tools for designing and development: In tool design flow, the tool suites like capability and usability should be considered. Analyzing tools as well evaluating tools effectively is crucial. Toolkit consists of required software and FPGA design, and development tools. Co-design is a term used to describe how these two tool groupings interact. The softcore processors and peripherals are in charge of parameterizing the implementation tools. They are also responsible for implementing other peripherals like processor buses, memory mapping and interrupt handlers. The software tools handle the compilation, linking, debugging and download to the target system.

Considerations for operating systems: The majority of embedded systems for processors with 32-bit incorporated in operating system to shorten the software cycle by giving it an abstraction interface level. The interconnection between the software and lower level hardware is possible by OS. A Board Support Package (BSP) is the usual name for this group of software components. The BSP may contain peripheral interrupt service routines and processor boot code, among other things. There are few issues to be addressed by OS like kernel size, latency caused due to interrupt, kernel size, set of services, and middleware featured collection.

Options and capacity for debugging: Without the proper tools and design access, the debugging stage of a design always leads to be iterative and may take up a major portion of a design time. Effective design debugging can eliminate weeks off the design process and schedule. Design efficiency considerations that are extremely crucial include robust debug features and capabilities.

Materials from the manufacturer and technical assistance: Another critical component in evaluating soft processor design is manufactures support. Key supporting components consists of: talks, tutorials, and exhibits, the availability of design specimen, reference code, and adequate documentation. The availability of regional and industrial technical resources as needed by specialist technical assistance in soft processor design for evaluating and examining boards with a wide enough functional scope. Device and tool availability, design question and response databases, documentation that is complete and current.

Based on key architectural aspects, a number of soft-core processors offered by different vendors and open-source communities are examined and contrasted. Additionally, a number of real-world instances of embedded devices using soft-core processors are compiled. Few examples of softcore processors are:

1. Altera Lattice Micro32: 32-bit microprocessor RISC uses Hardward Architecture
2. NIOS/NIOS11: 32-bit processor designed for Altera family. It is efficient for low cost FPGA application.
3. Xilinx PicoBlaze: 8-bit architecture Virtex4 family.
4. MicroBlaze: 32-bit instructions and issues new instruction every cycle modification preset 32-bit/64-bit.

These softcore processors provide memory and logic components as intellectual property during design of Systems on Chip (SoC). The MicroBlaze processor is a soft microprocessor that was primarily created for Xilinx FPGAs. Simply put, Xilinx FPGAs' general-purpose memory & logic fabric contains this processor. This processor features a RISC-based design that is comparable to the DLX architecture, and it includes a flexible interconnect system that enables it to serve a variety of embedded applications. The MicroBlaze uses a memory-mapped transaction bus with a master-slave facility as its primary Input/output (I/O) bus and Advanced eXtensible Interface (AXI).

The choice of MicroBlaze processor has following advantages: economical, supports configurability, provides high performance, and suitable for real time applications.

5.2 Sorters on RISC-V

Single-Instruction-Multiple Data (SIMD) directives can produce data-level parallelism. The majority of contemporary processors use SIMD as an instruction-level accelerator. The adaptability of RISC-V allows for the customization of instructions based on the application and the necessary accelerator devices. For the odd-even merge sort in [66], special instructions and a new template were created. By optimizing SIMD instructions, speed is also improved and the code length is reduced.

Soft-core CPUs expanded its acceptance and demand over many years. It is possible to synthesize these processor hardware description models utilizing a variety of semiconductor devices, including Programmable Logic Devices (PLD), Application Specific Integrated Circuits (ASIC), and Field Programmable Gate Arrays (FPGA). To get the best design trade-offs, designers can adapt their structures using soft-core processors to a particular application. By increasing the cache memory hierarchy's bandwidth in [66], the performance was enhanced. The softcore cache structure is bandwidth-optimized, with particularly broad blocks for the last-level cache, for the purpose of enhancing the speed of custom SIMD instructions. The use of FPGA in big data processing is unrivaled [67]. An intriguing hardware acceleration platform for a sizable number of database processes is the FPGA. Although their benefit in terms of overall performance for non-local data is rarely challenged, FPGAs are superior in terms of energy efficiency. A few of the FPGA disadvantages are described below, including the bandwidth constraint for data analytics application, the cost of communication disruptions, higher-end FPGAs [68], random cache memory access, and design consequences [69].

New instruction types, Verilog templates, an open source framework and high throughput were all used in [66]. It provides facility to customize SIMD instructions while focusing on communication and cache memory. Combining RISCV32I and RISCV32M improves the functionality of modified instructions in [66]. It offers effective FPGA implementation using BRAM.

The steps of a traditional sorting system are firstly, collecting data and accretion, then processing, dynamic and long-term storage, lastly sort and dispatch. Majority of the hardware sorting technique uses linear sorting strategies to preserve the in-order sorted list. This methodology has major drawback like not optimized solution and reduces throughput. Another constrain in sorting process is capacity usually designed for less number of data items. Taken any sorting methods, one data is fetched at a time even though hardware based sorting provides parallel execution to gain overall speedup. Hence, irrespective of sorting technique and hardware device, only one data is sorted at every clock cycle. In a pipelined fashion of execution, schedulers for data processing and arrival timings to be considered. The pipeline stall is due to unavailability of data for further processing and hence it cannot be advanced to next stage [70].

[70] presents linear sorter implementation systems on FPGAs and MicroBlaze processor. Systolic sorters and sorting networks both suffer from latency issues that are resolved by linear sorters. They are extremely adjustable due to their regular structure, making them an appropriate choice for streaming data.

Due to the fact that Bitonic sorting networks [18, 71] achieves improved throughput while working freely on available data sets and renders practically obsolete by this aspect. [71] introduced compare-swap unit for searching and sorting algorithms. This sorter technique provides low-latency in pipelining stages and well performed via parallelism technique. There are numerous sorting methods exist, including Bitonic sort, Odd-even sort, Bubble sort, Merge sort, and Insertion sort. These algorithms are implemented using Verilog HDL. Each of sorting methods has its own advantages and disadvantages, which are listed in [72].

To reduce the use of units and maintain low fragmentation, this article [73] developed a reconfigurable design based on SRAM. Including low-utilized LUTs to allow for reconfigurability. Furthermore, Configurable Hard Logics (CHLs) are utilized in conjunction with LUTs to increase the efficiency of reconfigurable design. These MiBench benchmarks and the Berkeley RISC-V processor are used to implement this design. LEON and DSP core processors are alternate to implement open source processors. RISC-V strength is for safety-critical applications and the LEON CPU for low power, reconfigurability is possible.

SecretBlaze [74] and Chisel [75] are two examples of effective soft core processors and are highly configurable. The application domain is not generic, and conventional reconfigurable architectures are power inefficient [76]– [79]. [73] suggests a reconfigurable architecture employing low utilization and fragmented functional units that focuses on effective area and power for soft core computers.

Benchmarks are used to identify the functional units with low utilization and fragmentation. The ideal modules for both soft and hard cores are Application Specific Integrated Circuit (ASIC) and Reconfigurable Unit (RU) modules. However, this methodology has some limitations, including the disregard for access patterns. The fundamental issue is Look Up Table (LUT) utilization, notwithstanding the fact that in broad circuits LUTs are underutilized for little input [80] [81]. Extension of RISC-V by including hardware-based division and multiplication operations to the open standard set presented in [82].

To allow M-extension with the least amount of overhead, this work proposed a multi-cycle execution unit of RVCoreP based on a basic fork-join structure. By assuming that instructions are processed in order, this architecture was designed with the RISC-V ISA supporting 32-bit soft processor in mind and was evaluated against several Benchmarks.

Depending on the application's need for multiplication and division/reminder instruction, the system designer should take care of the M-extension design over the RV32I. And it is discovered that RV32IM utilizes FPGA resources at a rate that is roughly 1.5 times higher than RV32I. Performance of DSP-based multiplier shows better than the iterative multipliers like the radix-4 booth multiplier.

The Xuantie-910 [83] is a RISC-V processor designed for 12-stage, 64-bit pipeline with out-of-order execution that produces highly effective vector processing, supports multi-core processors, and offers superior performance to its predecessor. For application-specific acceleration, the Alibaba Cloud data centers have implemented the Xuantie-910 FPGA (e.g., transaction through blockchain). The deployment of ASIC is intended for low cost SoC applications starting from IoT endpoints till the edge computing in cloud.

There are various factors considered while designing in work [84] like register file organization, encoding of instructions, pipeline operation, their functionalities, types, complexity of the decoder logic, data hazard detection, and access, data memory access, operating modes, the effects of branch instructions, control flow, and hardware resources for the execution unit. The processor was micro-architecture, tested on an FPGA platform, and synthesized using Blue-spec System Verilog on 65nm and 130nm TSMC technology nodes for ASIC.

Threats, also referred to as soft errors, are caused by bit flips in digital systems. This causes data corruption that goes undiscovered. The management of various soft faults by BOOM and Rocket processor is studied in [85]. The fault injection testing shows strong connections between two CPU cores. The processor cores with various ISAs do not exhibit this significant correlation characteristic. Based on this findings, an investigation will be conducted through a condensed set of fault injection experiments and a limited sequence of benchmark programmes. Additionally, it is possible to forecast how soft mistakes may affect a target processor core.

Utilizing a heuristic technique for choosing the programmes to be used for the fault injection trials on the processor core. It is possible to attain a high level of prediction accuracy with prediction errors of less than 7%. The same ISA system designs can be quickly evaluated for error resilience using this method.

[86] implemented on a three-stage pipelined FPGA with low complexity control circuitry. Furthermore, special instruction enhances the functionality of the current ISA as suggested to help in energy metering. This processor comprises a 3-stage pipeline, independent of write-back ports and a simple control architecture. Additionally, it offers some original guidelines for energy metering accumulation. In this work, utilizes the instructions that enhances the performance of energy accumulation in comparison to other designs.

Execution time overhead was eliminated by primarily synthesizing and deploying instrumented code in RISC-V and FPGA [87]. Where to place the tracing instructions in source code is determined by static analysis in fact afterwards, the processing time might be recorded through a logic analyzer. This creates overhead by the execution of the trace instructions, results in biggest flaw. This paper suggests a change to the RISC pipelined processor's architecture that gets rid of the penalty caused due to execution time caused by code instrumentation. Non-intrusive tracing can be enabled by executing sequence of instructions in a program.

Since RISC-V supports open source and is taped out on the 180nm TSMC process, it enables us to add additional instructions in the proposed work [88]. This study suggests that the main CPU directly accommodates the embedded FPGA (eFPGA). A direct connection between CPU and eFPGA allows quick swapping for the runtime instructions and easy for partial reconfiguration. There are multiple slots designed for the eFPGA system that helps the instructions to execute in parallel. Further this instruction can be merged to host sophisticated instructions. Implementation of instructions are quite flexible due to its feature like switching between instructions without halting processor and instructions with variable cycles can be executed. The LowRISC Ibex RISC-V core consists of logic blocks, DSP, Slices and register files. This feature enables the customized embed of FPGA.

The LowRISC Ibex RISC-V core is compact and has two pipeline stages, which uses less space. In this work [89] examined resource optimization. In comparison to using simply soft processors and out-of-order execution, RISC-V with FPGA enhances resource consumption. [89] proposed the RSD microprocessor, a new Out-of-Order (OoO) RISC-V softcore processor designed for an FPGA. A nonblocking cache, speculative scheduling, memory instruction execution and disambiguation, a memory predictor, and other aggressive OoO execution characteristics are supported by the RSD.

RISC-V includes attributes like adaptability, versatility, and this features are not yet available in the existing solutions, and it supports ISA without incurring any expenditures [90]. The MB-Lite, a non-RISC-V processor, was utilized to implement this ISA and was enhanced with new functionalities such caches, PCIe bus data transmission, a serial communication module (UART), counters and timers, and multi-cycle functional units. The main concern in this study is the design of a non-RISC-V core-based architecture for a RISC-V softcore processor that will be implemented on an FPGA logic device.

SecretBlaze [91] is a 32-bit RISC softcore processor with a five stage pipeline that is open source and appropriate for System On Chip (SOC) design. SecretBlaze uses the available instruction set from MicroBlaze softcore processors. It is quite flexible, balancing processing efficiency and space cost to satisfy the needs of embedded systems. This strategy raises the level of abstraction in hardware descriptions and offers efficient implementation.

5.3 Comparison-Free Sorter on MicroBlaze Architecture

FPGA core processors are considered to be intellectual property (IP). This Soft cores consists of design components that can be used in FPGA device. This section introduces the proposed processor's architecture. The main emphasis is on the modifications made to the MicroBlaze architecture and the RISC-V ISA implementation. The additional features and choices made in regards to the FPGA device has great impact. The CPU architecture overview is provided in this chapter to highlight the key structural changes. In the subsections that follow, each element is covered in further detail.

5.3.1 Optimization of Sorter

The proposed comparison free odd-even sort was compared to the different sorters, including Bitonic, Insertion, Selection, and Bubble sort. The characteristics used for the comparison are Number of slices, Number of LUT's, Number of utilized logics, Number of LUT Flip-flops, IO consumption, and finally Delay. All types of sorters listed in this chapter were designed to sort 4-, 8-, 16-, and 32-bit data. Table 5.1 highlights the proposed sorter's outcome with comparison of other sorters.

5.3.2 Overview of Architecture

MicroBlaze soft core processor is specifically designed for Xilinx FPGA. The implementation carried out in the main memory and logic blocks of FPGA. At each clock cycle, new

Table 5.1 Comparison of various parameters of existing sorters with the proposed Odd-Even Comparison-free sorter for different bit length

Data in Bit Size	Sorter Types	# of Slice Registers: (Out of 515200)	# of Slice LUTs: (Out of 257600)	# used as Logic (Out of 257600)	# of LUT Flip Flop pairs used (%)	Utilization of IO units (350)	Delay: (ns)
4 bits	Bitonic	72	219	221	31	68	2.874
	Proposed sorter	**70**	**168**	**168**	**30**	**68**	**2.147**
	Insertion	70	168	168	41	68	2.497
	Selection	79	214	216	33	68	3.338
	Bubble	76	235	236	31	68	3.433
8 bits	Bitonic	140	430	436	33	134	3.431
	Proposed sorter	**134**	**284**	**284**	**28**	**132**	**3.104**
	Insertion	138	637	640	32	132	3.409
	Selection	145	378	382	38	132	3.743
	Bubble	145	395	400	37	132	3.475
16 Bit	Bitonic	264	650	652	41	260	4.697
	Proposed sorter	**262**	**491**	**491**	**37**	**260**	**3.791**
	Insertion	274	1087	1097	45	260	5.607
	Selection	270	645	646	42	260	4.865
	Bubble	273	678	679	41	260	5.942
32 bits	Bitonic	518	1536	1536	44	516	5.786
	Proposed sorter	**521**	**1052**	**1052**	**42**	**518**	**4.445**
	Insertion	620	2777	2867	46	516	5.873
	Selection	530	1150	1155	46	56	4.899
	Bubble	533	1331	1338	48	516	6.125

instructions and data are sent out. Caches, pre-built peripherals like UART, timers, and counters, and assistance for multi-cycle functional units stand out. Based on this findings, the article solution focused on keeping the MicroBlaze properties, such as the techniques used and their robustness, in addition to implementing the RISC-V ISA.
Along with support for the RISC-V ISA, this architecture now has a sorter unit, which is seen as a crucial component for real-time applications. The MicroBlaze processor enables more than 70 design possibilities and is highly customizable. The Instruction or Data Cache, the Memory Management Unit, the Floating Point Unit, and other adjustable hardware components are displayed in this architecture together with other permanent hardware features.

The MicroBlaze softcore processors embedded with following components:

i. Soft core processor
ii. On-chip memory
iii. Bus interconnectors
iv. On-chip peripheral bus

A MicroBlaze processor system typically consists of a single processing core connected to local-memory and a system along with several MicroBlaze processors OPB peripherals and external memory.

The following features included in this architecture with the RISC-V ISA:

- The creation of a multiplier and a multi-cycle divider, as well as the support of extra functional units.
- After the ID stage, support for some instructions being executed out of sequence.
- Creation of a specific unit for handling and detecting conflicts brought on by the out-of-order execution and other structural risks.
- Adding a second writing port to the Register File will allow the non-memory instructions to be written back without passing through an additional stage, coming straight after the EX stage.

- Development of auxiliary devices (UART module, counter, timer, and data cache).
- For the purpose of maintaining the flow of instructions, a buffer that serves as a waiting queue between the EX and the MEM stage has been added. It stores memory request instructions there, until they move on to the MEM stage.

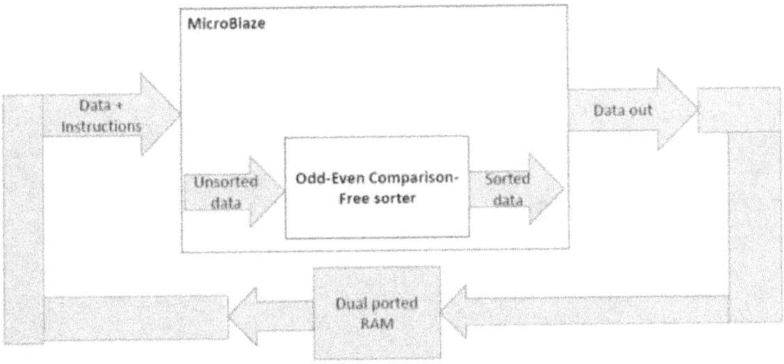

Figure 5.1: MicroBlaze Architecture Overview

The processing architecture of MicroBlaze, which incorporates an odd-even comparison-free sorter, is shown in Figure 5.1. Data and instructions are retrieved by MicroBlaze from the local memory (i.e RAM). The Odd-Even comparison-free sorter effectively sorts the unsorted data it receives from RAM by employing the sorter unit.

The MicroBlaze architecture, based on MIPS processors, is depicted in Figure 5.2. It features a pipeline of three stage with a modular implementation design as well as two different instruction and data memory. The 32-bit instruction is passed to the decode unit from the fetch stage, where it is decoded into an opcode, function, operands, and immediate. Additionally, present in this pipeline stage are the register file and control unit. The RISC-V register file contains 32 registers. In register zero, a special-purpose register, the constant value zero is kept. From the hardware's point of view, registers 1 through 31 perform normally. The same hardware description approach and signal naming standards were used to methodically create and specify each phase in its own component. The Write-Back stage and instruction decode stage was built in the same component due to its connectivity to the Register File.

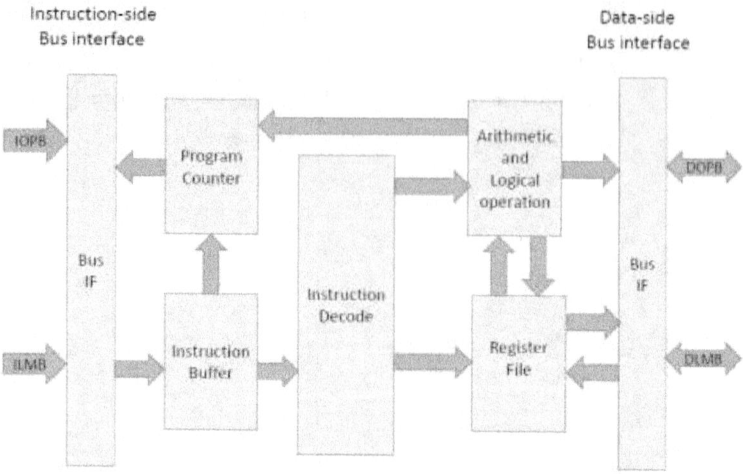

Figure 5.2: MicroBlaze Architecture with 3-stage Pipeline

5.3.3 RISC-V ISA

A system may only desire to employ a subset of the instructions available in CISC or certain RISC ISAs, but the CPU for these systems must still support the original larger instruction set. A basic integer ISA for RISC-V is available in 32, 64, and 128-bit versions (RV32, RV64, and RV128, respectively). Additionally, it offers optional extensions, giving users the freedom to develop only what is required for a given application. The RISC-V ISA can be used to realize high-performance, energy-efficient systems regardless of the microarchitecture (i.e., out-of-order) or implementation technology (i.e., FPGA, ASIC, custom hardware) used.

The two important features of RISC-V ISA are as follows:

1. Expandable and Configurability: The current processor supports ISA with a designated set of instructions. The system should support the new ISA added to it without compromising performance. Due to insufficient opcode for the new set of instructions, including additional instructions to an ISA may, in the extreme, necessitate a total

redesign. On the other hand, RISC-V has been built in such a way that it can be extended to new or future instructions.

It is possible to configure RISC-V with both base and extended instruction sets. Here, extension sets include floating-point operations with single-precision, double-precision, quad-precision, and integer multiply/divide and atomic, among others. There are enough operation codes set aside for upcoming instructions in addition to the full extension sets. Moreover, depending on the desired computing domain, the RISC-V ISA can be designed. As a result, one can consider the RISC-V ISA to be a "family" of processors. This processor includes data path lengths and other functionalities.

2. Rapid growth in ecosystem: The software/hardware that enable processor configuration to quickly integrate additional devices/platforms are referred to as an ISA environment. An ISA design consists of a number of software tools, including operating systems, compilers, debuggers, and ISA simulators. The GCC/LLVM compiler, Linux OS, and other applications are part of the RISC-V software ecosystem.

Because new formats require rewriting the parsing of each instruction, the modifications needed to implement the RISC-V ISA were preferably made in the instruction decoder. The MicroBlaze ISA only supports Type A (for register-register instructions) and Type B instructions (used for register-immediate operations). Contrarily, the ISA in RISC-V offers six distinct categories of instructions. New entries were subsequently added to the decoder in order to parse the new type of instructions.

Each instruction type is given a distinct opcode since instructions of the same sort share the same opcode/pneumonic. Once the typeset has been established, the individual instruction is then identified and the operands are acquired. This lowers the barrier to entry for creating a RISC-V implementation and boosts security. There are no mysterious instructions when running code because all instructions are visible to the user.

5.3.4 Memory Organization

Data and instructions are kept in separate memory in a Harvard architecture. While this architecture allows for simultaneous access to data and instructions, it is not possible to merge the program and data addressing areas. Hence, making it impossible to load a new program as data before executing it. Because each program must be transferred before being run, this processor is designed to be used as a slave. In addition to supporting instructions and data storage, the CPU also supports peripheral that are a part of the address space. Memory instructions are processed by the address decoder and well routed in accordance with the address map that can access them.

5.3.5 Instruction Memory

Due to the absence of an instruction cache, the program instructions are kept in Block Random Access Memory (BRAM). A Peripheral Component Interconnect express (PCIe) port and a port for retrieving instructions from the CPU should both be present on the memory. The PCIe port should be ready to receive and transfer data between the memory and peripheral components, respectively.

A BRAM generator [92] that supports a variety of RAM types and has scalable capacities is available from Xilinx through the Vivado's IP Catalog. Given that it provides two read and write ports for separate addresses operating simultaneously, as well as two independent clocks, the Dual-Port BRAM is the ideal choice for the design. It is possible to connect one of the ports to receive data sent over PCIe in this manner, but due to implementation limitations, this interface must be compatible with AXI4. This work used Xilinx AXI Block RAM Controller IP to convert between the two interfaces because BRAMs and AXI. The interfaces are mostly incompatible. The connection technique of the MicroBlaze is adaptable enough to support a variety of embedded applications.

The primary Input/Output bus of MicroBlaze and the Advanced eXtensible Interface (AXI) link, is a master-slave transaction bus that is system memory mapped. The 32-bit MicroBlaze

Core Processor is closely related to the timer, sorter, controller UART connectivity, local memory, and debug interface.

The MicroBlaze processor features a RISC-based engine that contains a register file based on 32-bit LUT RAM using distinct instructions for memory & data access. It also supports 32-bit bus width. This processor is compatible with on-chip Block RAM and external memory. Peripherals connected to the processor are more compatible with IBM PowerPC on Virtex-II Pro. This MicroBlaze processor gives entire freedom to combine memory, peripheral, and interface capabilities to create the precise system you need on a single FPGA at a lower cost. The connections between the Dual-Port BRAM-based instruction memory and the AXI Block RAM Controller are shown in Figure 5.3. It is represented by two separate clock signals, one from PCIe logic and the other from the specialized core clock. Asynchronous serial data transfer is available with AXI UARTlite. The AXI interface is based on the AXI4-Lite specification, uses a single transmit and receive channel (full duplex). The Odd-Even sorter unit is coupled to the MicroBlaze soft processor through the AXI interface.

5.3.6 Performance Analysis

Usually HDL/RTL design abstraction used for chip design. In recent days, an alternative level of abstraction for designing processor is High-Level Synthesis (HLS). In hardware design this approaches have recently grown in favor. With HLS, the intended behavior is specified in a C/C++ software programme. The programme is then run on a common microprocessor after being compiled (for instance, using gcc). This is done to ensure that it is functional and correct. Using HLS, high level language like C, C++ programs are by default compiled into Register Transfer Logic. HLS make devices accessible to persons with only software expertise and enables hardware creation to take place at a higher degree of abstraction. For the purpose of implementing hardware accelerators, the combination of FPGAs and HLS is particularly potent.

The Vertex-4 with the series 4VLX40-12 used in this simulation. The MicroBlaze is capable operating up to 200 MHz. Depending on how the processor is set up, a MicroBlaze soft processor can take anywhere from 900 to 2,600 Look-Up Tables (LUTs) to implement. The

Xilinx Artix7 "XC7A200T-2FBG6762" MicroBlaze softcore FPGA was used to model and synthesize the proposed Odd-Even Comparison-Free sorter principally at 100MHz frequency.

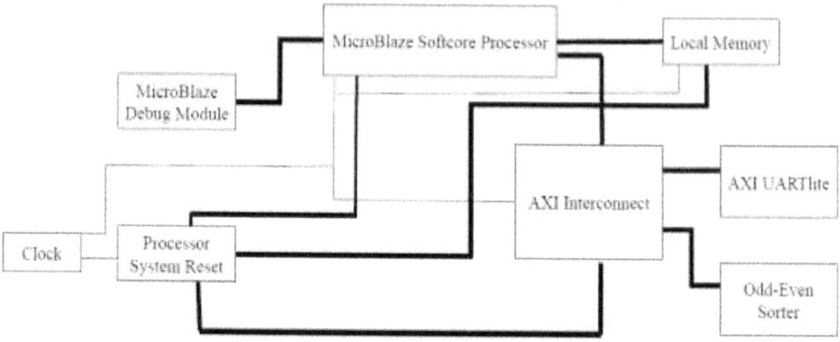

Figure 5.3: Connections between the Core, Local Memory, AXI Block RAM Controller, and Interconnect (implemented using a Dual Ported RAM IP)

The devices used for the proposed sorting on the softcore FPGA, open RISC, and Rocket core are shown in Table 5.2. A processor has been synthesized using the UMC 90nm and Cadence Encounter RTL compiler. Table 5.3 shows the amount of logic block resource utilization of MicroBlaze Softcore Processor.

Table 5.2 Device utilization of MicroBlaze Softcore Processor

Selected Parameters	Proposed softcore	Open RISC [27]	Rocket Core[28]
# of Slice Registers	1609	1287	1342
# of Slice LUTs	1327	1784	1376

Table 5.3 Resource-Utilization of Logic Blocks

MMCM	BUFG	I/O	BRAM	FF	LUTRAM	LUT
10%	13%	1%	2%	1%	1%	1%

In Table 5.4, the outcomes of work presented in this chapter is odd-even comparison-free sorter. The summarized parameters with respect to the IOB, number of slices, number of LUTs, number of logic gates, number of registers, and number of muxes are considered. Tests are conducted at a 100MHz frequency. Seven elements were taken into consideration when sorting the data. N is therefore always equal to 7. Therefore, the overall length for 32-bit numbers is 224 bits.

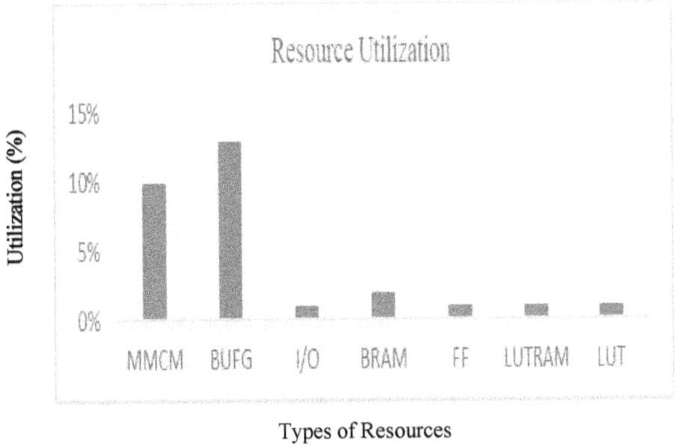

Figure 5.4: Resource-Utilization of Comparison-free sorters

Table 5.4 Resource-Utilization of Odd-Even Comparison-Free Sorter

Sorting Technique	IOB	# of slices	# of LUT's	# of Registers	# of LUT Flipflops	Muxes
Odd-even comparison free merge sort(proposed)	164	84	320	130	520	80

Power is a crucial indicator of a processor's performance in an embedded system because it affects the core's thermal demands and battery usage. Power for the design being tested is displayed hierarchically for the modules in the Xilinx MicroBlaze. The power consumption of different on-chip components, including Input/Output, BRAM, static power, Muxes, Registers, and other logic components, is shown in Figure 5.5. The overall power consumption for sorting elements is 25.9%, as seen in the graph.

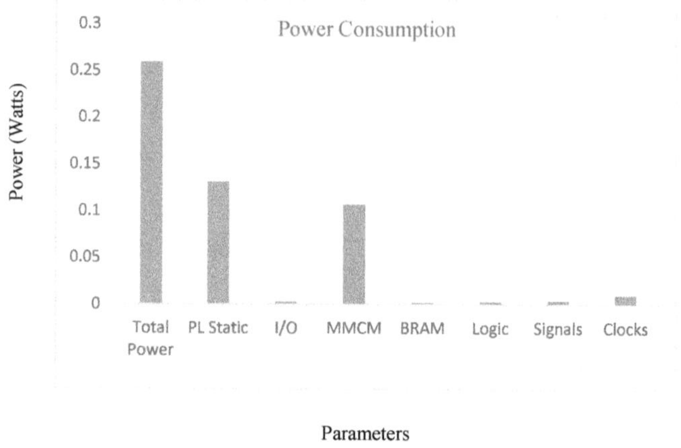

Figure 5.5: Power-Consumption

Table 5.5 provides information on the power usage by various blocks in watts. And Table 5.6 displays the delays incurred by the data and instruction paths.

Table 5.5 Power-Consumption by various blocks

Total Power	Static Power	I/O	MMCM	BRAM	Logic	Signals	Clocks
0.259	0.131	0.003	0.107	0.002	0.003	0.004	0.01

Table 5.6 Maximum path delays

Data Path Delay	Destination Clock Delay	Source Clock Delay	Slack (MET)
2.580ns	3.709ns	4.162ns	14.037ns

Two functions with four inputs each make up a slice, together with carry logic, arithmetic logic, storage logic, and a function multiplexer. The flip-flop in Slice has a variety of functioning modes that can be selected, including FF or Latch, synchronous or asynchronous reset, reset high or low effective, etc. The detailed slice logic resource utilization is depicted in Table 5.7. The major resource utilized in MicroBlaze architecture is slice LUTs.

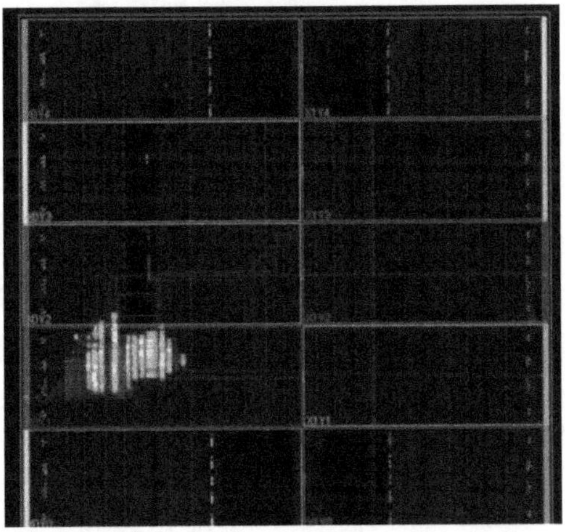

Figure 5.6: RV32I Sorting illustration for 7 elements

Table 5.7 Slice Logic and its utilization

Slice Type	Used	Available	% of Utilization
Slice LUTs	1465	133800	1.09
LUT as Logic	1327	133800	0.99
LUT as Memory	138	46200	0.3
Slice Registers	1609	267600	0.6
Muxes	141	66900	0.21

An optional secondary clock source and clocksel functionality are displayed by the clock wizard- Mixed-Mode Clock Management (MMCM or PLL). A clock buffer called BUFG has a single clock input and output. Compiler used in FPGA adds a universal global clock buffer (BUFG) automatically whenever an input given to the device. Table 5.8 Clocking utilization of BUFGCLK and MMCME.

The two most important criteria for evaluating any CPU design are performance and power consumption. Table 5.9 and 5.10 reports the values for the chip (MicroBlaze) power utilization. The power used by the clock propagation signal is known as clock power. The term "logic power" describes the combined and sequential logic blocks' power usage. The power used by the interior wiring is referred to as signal power.

Table 5.8 Clock Utilization

Site Type	Used	Available	% of Utilization
BUFGCLK	4	32	12.5
MMCME	1	10	10

Table 5.9 Report on Power

Total On-Chip Power (W)	0.259
Dynamic (W)	0.128
Device Static (W)	0.131
Effective TJA (C/W)	1.9
Max Ambient (C)	84.5

Table 5.10 On-Chip Components

On-Chip	Power Utilization
Clocks	0.01
Slice Logic	0.003
LUT as Logic	0.002
Signals	0.004
Block RAM	0.002
MMCM	0.107
I/O	0.003
Static Power	0.131
Total	0.259

The power used by the IOs through IOBs is referred to as IO power. The standby power of the chip (FPGA), also known as quiescent power, is referred to as leakage power. By limiting the implemented instructions to those pertinent to certain applications, MicroBlaze processors significantly minimize the power consumption and usage of hardware resources. The most recent Xilinx Vivado Design Suite results are used as the foundation for the power estimations.

Power consumption by various modules are listed in Table 5.11.

Table 5.11 Power distribution for Modules

Name	Power(W)
sort_microblaze_wrapper	0.128
sort_microblaze_i	0.128
clk_wiz_1 (clock wizard)	0.111
Inst (element instances)	0.111
microblaze_0	0.011
U0 (rebuild cell)	0.011
microblaze_0_local_memory	0.002
lmb_bram	0.002
sort_ip_0	0.001

5.4 Summary

Here, an optimized comparison-free even-odd sorter for the RISC-V architecture was proposed. After comparing it to a number of factors, including memory, power usage, and resource utilization, it was established that it was capable of superior performance. It was decided to use a comparison-free Odd-Even sorter and to implement it using the MicroBlaze architecture. By using the suggested strategy, it was possible to decrease both the area needed for implementation and the active memory range requirement. The suggested sorter proves that it has the ability to sort any kind of asymmetries and produces output that is entirely sorted. On a 100MHz Xilinx Artix7 "XC7A200T-2FBG6762" MicroBlaze softcore FPGA, the sorter was successfully constructed.

Chapter 6

Conclusion

This thesis work investigates the use of dedicated hardware (FPGA) to speed up in-memory database processes. Online analytical processing and data mining have become more common database workloads than just Online Transaction Processing (OLTP). An exploration of hardware architectures for sorting acceleration is a crucial part of applications related to data center acceleration. Bitonic sorter, bubble sorter, and odd-even sorter are appropriate sorting methods for hardware implementation. Designing sorting strategies for hardware implementation emphasizes performance enhancements and minimizing power consumption.

The clock gating technique employed on three different hardware sorting and this resulted in low power consumption. The trade-off factors like timing, area, and power consumption is analyzed for all three sorters. Contrasting to the proposed sorters with clock gating to conventional (non-clock gated) sorting circuits, the dynamic power/energy consumption is reduced by 47.51%. This clock gated sorters lowers overall dynamic power consumption with increasing frequency of operation. This is compared and contrasted on all three conventional sorters.

Multi-Vth libraries are used to further reduce the critical path or improve frequency. Comparative results are presented between the most recent low power sorting systems and the clock gated sorting architectures. Without compromising the reduction in dynamic power consumption obtained through clock gating, multi-Vth implementation will reduce the critical path. The suggested clock gated sorters consume 47.5% less dynamic power than traditional (non-clock gated) sorting circuits.

The proposed clock gated sorters' dynamic power consumption gradually decreases with higher operating frequencies, according to analysis of the clock gating technique on sorters for a variety of frequencies. When compared to more traditional techniques, the recommended clock gated strategy dramatically reduces the dynamic power consumption of three extensively used sorting algorithms.

To sort N elements, a modified Odd-Even method is proposed. The proposed technique is comparison-free odd-even sorter. The proposed sorting complexity is used to indicate sorting speed, i.e O(N). The enlarged even-odd sorter is tested and validated by implementing it on Virtex-7-configured FPGAs, which can operate at 224 MHz. From the simulation results, it clearly shows that even the smallest resource allocation was sufficient to defeat several modern hardware-based categorization techniques with only minimal sorting delays.

An efficient comparison-free even-odd sorter for the RISC-V architecture implemented in this work. After comparing it to a number of factors, including memory, power usage, and resource utilization, it was established that it was capable of higher performance. It was decided to use a comparison-free Odd-Even sorter and to implement it using the MicroBlaze architecture. The proposed sorter verifies that it is capable of sorting any kind of asymmetrical data and produces output that is fully sorted. The Xilinx Artix7 "XC7A200T-2FBG6762" MicroBlaze softcore FPGA at 100MHz successfully implemented the proposed sorter.

Hence, from the result analysis it is clear that hardware accelerators improve performance of the system in terms of power consumption, processing time and memory usage. In chapter 3, the low power techniques like clock gating and multi-Vth are used to reduce the power consumption and delay. The chapter 4 presents the resource utilization for the comparison-free sorters which consumes less resource compared to other sorting logic. The chapter 5 illustrated advantage of using RISC-V architecture implementing comparison-free sorter on MicroBlaze softcore processor.

Chapter 7

Future Work

The work presented in this thesis can be extended for implementing low power sorter techniques to larger input data. Applying Low power techniques to different kind of sorters. Currently, the Xilinx Artix-7 FPGA's hardware resources were fully utilized by the benchmarks shown in this work. Larger data can be benchmarked on the proposed designs if a larger FPGA devices and a more potent computer are available to shorten compile times. There are some crucial places where sorting accelerator implementation might be enhanced. There is room for more hardware to optimize the accelerator because so little of the available reconfigurable area is being utilized.

Integrating the High Throughput comparison-free Sorting Accelerator into current software, such as a SQL database, would make for an interesting area for further study. Also implementing comparison-free sorter on various sorting philosophy like Bitonic sort, bubble sort and selection sort. A more thorough performance comparison between systems with and without this accelerator can be made when this is included into real-world use cases.

Executing out-of-order instructions in RISC-V processor is one of the challenge. Addition to this, a hardware sorting unit is implemented on RISC-V processor. An in-order processor was employed in this work. The proposed sorting logic cannot be operated concurrently with other instructions in an in-order processor. Generally, CPU converts the pipelining stages into an out-of-order processor instruction. This would enable full utilization of the pipelined hardware sorting unit.

Chapter 6

Conclusion

This thesis work investigates the use of dedicated hardware (FPGA) to speed up in-memory database processes. Online analytical processing and data mining have become more common database workloads than just Online Transaction Processing (OLTP). An exploration of hardware architectures for sorting acceleration is a crucial part of applications related to data center acceleration. Bitonic sorter, bubble sorter, and odd-even sorter are appropriate sorting methods for hardware implementation. Designing sorting strategies for hardware implementation emphasizes performance enhancements and minimizing power consumption.

The clock gating technique employed on three different hardware sorting and this resulted in low power consumption. The trade-off factors like timing, area, and power consumption is analyzed for all three sorters. Contrasting to the proposed sorters with clock gating to conventional (non-clock gated) sorting circuits, the dynamic power/energy consumption is reduced by 47.51%. This clock gated sorters lowers overall dynamic power consumption with increasing frequency of operation. This is compared and contrasted on all three conventional sorters.

Multi-Vth libraries are used to further reduce the critical path or improve frequency. Comparative results are presented between the most recent low power sorting systems and the clock gated sorting architectures. Without compromising the reduction in dynamic power consumption obtained through clock gating, multi-Vth implementation will reduce the critical path. The suggested clock gated sorters consume 47.5% less dynamic power than traditional (non-clock gated) sorting circuits.

The proposed clock gated sorters' dynamic power consumption gradually decreases with higher operating frequencies, according to analysis of the clock gating technique on sorters for a variety of frequencies. When compared to more traditional techniques, the recommended clock gated strategy dramatically reduces the dynamic power consumption of three extensively used sorting algorithms.

Chapter 7

Future Work

The work presented in this thesis can be extended for implementing low power sorter techniques to larger input data. Applying Low power techniques to different kind of sorters. Currently, the Xilinx Artix-7 FPGA's hardware resources were fully utilized by the benchmarks shown in this work. Larger data can be benchmarked on the proposed designs if a larger FPGA devices and a more potent computer are available to shorten compile times. There are some crucial places where sorting accelerator implementation might be enhanced. There is room for more hardware to optimize the accelerator because so little of the available reconfigurable area is being utilized.

Integrating the High Throughput comparison-free Sorting Accelerator into current software, such as a SQL database, would make for an interesting area for further study. Also implementing comparison-free sorter on various sorting philosophy like Bitonic sort, bubble sort and selection sort. A more thorough performance comparison between systems with and without this accelerator can be made when this is included into real-world use cases.

Executing out-of-order instructions in RISC-V processor is one of the challenge. Addition to this, a hardware sorting unit is implemented on RISC-V processor. An in-order processor was employed in this work. The proposed sorting logic cannot be operated concurrently with other instructions in an in-order processor. Generally, CPU converts the pipelining stages into an out-of-order processor instruction. This would enable full utilization of the pipelined hardware sorting unit.

To sort N elements, a modified Odd-Even method is proposed. The proposed technique is comparison-free odd-even sorter. The proposed sorting complexity is used to indicate sorting speed, i.e O(N). The enlarged even-odd sorter is tested and validated by implementing it on Virtex-7-configured FPGAs, which can operate at 224 MHz. From the simulation results, it clearly shows that even the smallest resource allocation was sufficient to defeat several modern hardware-based categorization techniques with only minimal sorting delays.

An efficient comparison-free even-odd sorter for the RISC-V architecture implemented in this work. After comparing it to a number of factors, including memory, power usage, and resource utilization, it was established that it was capable of higher performance. It was decided to use a comparison-free Odd-Even sorter and to implement it using the MicroBlaze architecture. The proposed sorter verifies that it is capable of sorting any kind of asymmetrical data and produces output that is fully sorted. The Xilinx Artix7 "XC7A200T-2FBG6762" MicroBlaze softcore FPGA at 100MHz successfully implemented the proposed sorter.

Hence, from the result analysis it is clear that hardware accelerators improve performance of the system in terms of power consumption, processing time and memory usage. In chapter 3, the low power techniques like clock gating and multi-Vth are used to reduce the power consumption and delay. The chapter 4 presents the resource utilization for the comparison-free sorters which consumes less resource compared to other sorting logic. The chapter 5 illustrated advantage of using RISC-V architecture implementing comparison-free sorter on MicroBlaze softcore processor.

www.ingramcontent.com/pod-product-compliance
Lightning Source LLC
LaVergne TN
LVHW021736071126
851857LV00040B/1461